THE IT4IT™

C000092199

The Open Group Publications available from Van Haren Publishing

The TOGAF Series:
TOGAF® Version 9.1
TOGAF® Version 9.1 – A Pocket Guide
TOGAF® 9 Foundation Study Guide, 3rd Edition
TOGAF® 9 Certified Study Guide, 3rd Edition

The Open Group Series:
The IT4IT™ Reference Architecture, Version 2.0 – A Pocket Guide
Cloud Computing for Business – The Open Group Guide
ArchiMate® 2.1 – A Pocket Guide
ArchiMate® 2.1 Specification
ArchiMate® 2 Certification – Study Guide

The Open Group Security Series:
Open Information Security Management Maturity Model (O-ISM3)
Open Enterprise Security Architecture (O-ESA)
Risk Management – The Open Group Guide
The Open FAIR™ Body of Knowledge – A Pocket Guide

All titles are available to purchase from:
www.opengroup.org
www.vanharen.net
and also many international and online distributors.

The IT4IT™ Reference Architecture, Version 2.0

A POCKET GUIDE

Prepared by Andrew Josey et al.

Title:	The IT4IT™ Reference Architecture, Version 2.0 – A Pocket Guide
Series:	The Open Group Series
A Publication of:	The Open Group
Author:	Andrew Josey.
Publisher:	Van Haren Publishing, Zaltbommel, www.vanharen.net
ISBN Hardcopy:	978 94 018 0030 3
ISBN eBook:	978 94 018 0588 9
ISBN ePUB:	978 94 018 0589 6
Edition:	First edition, first impression, October 2015
	First edition, second impression, November 2015
Layout and Cover Design:	CO2 Premedia, Amersfoort – NL
Copyright:	© 2015, The Open Group
	All rights reserved

The views expressed in this Pocket Guide are not necessarily those of any particular member of The Open Group.

In the event of any discrepancy between text in this document and the official IT4IT documentation, the IT4IT documentation remains the authoritative version for certification, testing by examination, and other purposes. The official IT4IT documentation can be obtained online at www.opengroup.org/bookstore/catalog/c155.htm.

The IT4IT™ Reference Architecture, Version 2.0 - A Pocket Guide

Document Number: G154

Published by The Open Group, October 2015.

Comments relating to the material contained in this document may be submitted to:

The Open Group
Apex Plaza
Reading
Berkshire, RG1 1AX
United Kingdom

or by electronic mail to: ogspecs@opengroup.org

Contents

Preface

This Document

This document is the Pocket Guide for the IT4IT™ Reference Architecture, Version 2.0, an Open Group Standard. It is designed to provide a reference for Business Managers, IT professionals, practitioners, and IT leaders.

The IT Value Chain and IT4IT Reference Architecture represent the IT service lifecycle in a new and powerful way. They provide the missing link between industry standard best practice guides and the technology framework and tools that power the IT service management ecosystem. The IT Value Chain and IT4IT Reference Architecture are a new foundation on which to base your IT operating model. Together, they deliver a blueprint to accelerate IT's transition to becoming a service broker to the business. They also address strategic challenges brought about by mobility, cloud, big data, security, and Bring Your Own Device (BYOD).

This allows organizations to:
- Focus on the true role of IT: to deliver services that make the company more competitive.
- Support the multi-sourced service economy, enabling new experiences in driving the self-sourcing of services that power innovation.

The intended audiences for this Pocket Guide includes:
- Individuals who require a basic understanding of the IT Value Chain and IT4IT Reference Architecture
- IT Professionals who are responsible for delivering services in a way that is flexible, traceable, and cost-effective
- IT Professionals/Practitioners who are focused on instrumenting the IT management landscape
- IT leaders who are concerned about the nature and appropriateness of their operating model

A prior knowledge of IT service management is advantageous but not required.

The Pocket Guide is structured as follows:

- Chapter 1 provides an introduction to this Pocket Guide, the IT4IT Reference Architecture, the structure of the IT4IT standard, and the positioning of the IT4IT standard in the standards landscape.
- Chapter 2 describes the IT Value Chain and IT4IT Reference Architecture concepts, including Value Streams.
- Chapter 3 describes the Strategy to Portfolio (S2P) Value Stream.
- Chapter 4 describes the Requirement to Deploy (R2D) Value Stream.
- Chapter 5 describes the Request to Fulfill (R2F) Value Stream.
- Chapter 6 describes the Detect to Correct (D2C) Value Stream.
- Appendix A summarizes the differences between the IT4IT Reference Architecture and ITIL.
- Appendix B includes the glossary of terms.
- Appendix C includes acronyms and abbreviations used in this Pocket Guide.

About IT4IT™

- IT4IT, an evolving Open Group standard, provides a vendor-neutral, technology-agnostic, and industry-agnostic reference architecture for managing the business of IT, enabling insight for continuous improvement.
- IT4IT provides the capabilities for managing the business of IT that will enable IT execution across the entire Value Chain in a better, faster, cheaper way with less risk.
- IT4IT is industry-independent to solve the same problems for everyone.
- IT4IT is designed for existing landscapes and accommodates future IT paradigms.

Conventions Used in this Pocket Guide

The following conventions are used throughout this Pocket Guide in order to help identify important information and avoid confusion over the intended meaning.

- Ellipsis (…)
  Indicates a continuation; such as an incomplete list of example items, or a continuation from preceding text.
- **Bold**
  Used to highlight specific terms.
- *Italics*
  Used for emphasis. May also refer to other external documents.

Readers should note that due to the limited number of colors used in this Pocket Guide, the model diagrams use a different color scheme to the official IT4IT documentation.

In addition to typographical conventions, the following conventions are used to highlight segments of text:

 A Note box is used to highlight useful or interesting information.

About The Open Group

The Open Group is a global consortium that enables the achievement of business objectives through IT standards. With more than 500 member organizations, The Open Group has a diverse membership that spans all sectors of the IT community – customers, systems and solutions suppliers, tool vendors, integrators, and consultants, as well as academics and researchers – to:

- Capture, understand, and address current and emerging requirements, and establish policies and share best practices

- Facilitate interoperability, develop consensus, and evolve and integrate specifications and open source technologies
- Offer a comprehensive set of services to enhance the operational efficiency of consortia
- Operate the industry's premier certification service

Further information on The Open Group is available at www.opengroup.org.

The Open Group publishes a wide range of technical documentation, most of which is focused on development of Open Group Standards and Guides, but which also includes white papers, technical studies, certification and testing documentation, and business titles. Full details and a catalog are available at www.opengroup.org/bookstore.

Readers should note that updates – in the form of Corrigenda – may apply to any publication. This information is published at www.opengroup.org/corrigenda.

About the Authors

Andrew Josey, The Open Group

Andrew Josey is Director of Standards within The Open Group. He is currently managing the standards process for The Open Group, and has recently led the standards development projects for the ArchiMate® Model Exchange File Format Standard, the ArchiMate® 2.1 Specification and the TOGAF® 9.1 Standard, IEEE Std 1003.1 2013 Edition (POSIX®), and the core specifications of the Single UNIX® Specification, Version 4. He is a member of the IEEE, USENIX, UKUUG, and the Association of Enterprise Architects (AEA).

Sylvain Marie, Arismore

Sylvain Marie is Project Director and Lead IT4IT Architect at Arismore, a consulting company involved in digital transformation. He is also in charge of the IT operational excellence offer within Arismore. He has been involved in IT service management projects from process design to tools implementation in large international enterprises for over 20 years He is a member of itSMF, The Open Group IT4IT Forum, and is ITIL and TOGAF certified. Within the itSMF, he is co-author of a white paper on "Transforming IT into a Service Provider" and has recently led a work stream on "Architecting the Information System of IT".

Charles (Charlie) Betz, Armstrong Process Group

Charlie Betz is the founder of Digital Management Academy LLC, a training, advisory, and consulting firm focused on new approaches to managing the "business of IT". He spent 6 years at Wells Fargo as VP and Enterprise Architect for IT Portfolio Management and Systems Management. He has held analyst, architect, and application manager positions for AT&T, Best Buy, Target, EMA, and Accenture, specializing in IT management, Cloud, and Enterprise Architecture. He has served as an ITIL reviewer and COBIT author. Currently, he is active in The Open

Group IT4IT Forum representing Armstrong Process Group. Charlie is an adjunct faculty member at the University of St. Thomas, and lives in Minneapolis, Minnesota with wife Sue and son Keane.

Christopher Davis, University of South Florida

Chris is Professor of Information Systems at the University of South Florida. His academic career spans 26 years, prior to which he spent 18 years in roles as an analyst and project manager in public sector and corporate organizations in the UK and Europe. Chris is particularly noted for his work on sensemaking in design. His work has been published in a range of outlets including *Communications of the ACM* and the *MIS Quarterly*. He is a Fellow of the British Computer Society, a Senior Member of IEEE, and served until recently as Associate Editor of the *European Journal of Information Systems*. Chris currently serves as the Chairman of The Open Group IT4IT Forum.

Lars Rossen, Hewlett-Packard

Lars Rossen is a Distinguished Technologist, and Chief Architect of the IT4IT initiative in Hewlett-Packard. He was part of the inception of the IT4IT initiative and constructed the first version of the IT4IT architecture. He leads the initiative that aligns and integrates all of the Hewlett-Packard management tools using IT4IT as the reference. Lars has been working on IT and Service Provider management systems and software for 20 years. Lars has a PhD in Computer Science, an MSc in Engineering, and an MBA in Technology Management. He currently lives in Denmark.

Trademarks

ArchiMate®, DirecNet®, Making Standards Work®, OpenPegasus®, The Open Group®, TOGAF®, UNIX®, and the Open Brand ("X" logo) are registered trademarks and Boundaryless Information Flow™, Build with Integrity Buy with Confidence™, Dependability Through Assuredness™, FACE™, IT4IT™, Open Platform 3.0™, Open Trusted Technology Provider™, UDEF™, and the Open "O" logo and The Open Group Certification logo are trademarks of The Open Group in the United States and other countries.

CMMI® is registered in the US Patent and Trademark Office by Carnegie Mellon University.

COBIT® is a registered trademark of the Information Systems Audit and Control Association (ISACA) and the IT Governance Institute.

eTOM® is a registered trademark of the TM Forum.

ITIL® is a registered trademark of AXELOS Ltd.

OASIS™ and TOSCA™ are trademarks of OASIS.

OMG®, Unified Modeling Language®, and UML®, are registered trademarks of the Object Management Group, Inc. in the United States and/or other countries.

All other brands, company, and product names are used for identification purposes only and may be trademarks that are the sole property of their respective owners.

Acknowledgements

The Open Group gratefully acknowledges:

- Past and present members of The Open Group IT4IT™ Forum for developing the IT4IT Reference Architecture and additional associated materials.
- The following reviewers of this document:
  - Steve Else
  - Mike Fulton
  - Steve Philp
  - Bart Verbrugge
  - Erik Witte

References

The following documents are referenced in this Pocket Guide:

- ArchiMate® 2.1 Specification, Open Group Standard (C13L), December 2013, published by The Open Group; refer to: www.opengroup.org/bookstore/catalog/c13l.htm.
- M. Porter: Competitive Advantage: Creating and Sustaining Superior Performance, ISBN: 978-0684841465, Free Press; 1st Edition (June 1998).
- TOGAF Version 9.1 (English version), Open Group Standard, available online at www.opengroup.org/architecture/togaf9-doc/arch, and also available as TOGAF Version 9.1 "The Book" (ISBN: 978 90 8753 6794, G116) at www.opengroup.org/bookstore/catalog/g116.htm.

Chapter 1
Introduction

This Pocket Guide provides a first introduction to the IT4IT Reference Architecture, Version 2.0, an Open Group Standard. It will be of interest to individuals who require a basic understanding of the IT Value Chain and the IT4IT Reference Architecture, and IT professionals and IT leaders who are concerned with – or about – their operating model.

This chapter provides a brief overview of the standard.

Topics addressed in this chapter include:
- An introduction to the IT4IT Reference Architecture
- The benefits of using the IT4IT Reference Architecture
- The structure and constituent parts of the IT4IT Reference Architecture
- The relationship of IT4IT to other Open Group standards and to other industry frameworks and methodologies

1.1 An Introduction to the IT4IT Reference Architecture

The Open Group IT4IT Reference Architecture standard comprises a reference architecture and value chain-based operating model for managing the business of IT. The operating model defined by the standard serves the digital enterprise with support for real-world use-cases (e.g., Cloud-sourcing, Agile, DevOps, and service brokering) as well as embracing and complementing existing process frameworks and methodologies (e.g., ITIL, COBIT, SAFe, and TOGAF).

It offers great value to any company that takes managing the business of IT seriously, and especially those with an interest in business and IT transitions. It allows the IT function within an organization to achieve the same level of business discipline, predictability, and efficiency as other functions in the business.

The standard is focused on defining, sourcing, consuming, and managing IT services by looking holistically at the entire IT Value Chain. While existing frameworks and standards have placed their main emphasis on process, this standard is process-agnostic, focused instead on the data needed to manage a service through its lifecycle. It then describes the functional components (software) that are required to produce and consume the data. Once integrated together, a system of record fabric for IT management is created that ensures full visibility and traceability of the service from cradle to grave.

IT4IT provides an Information Model
It is important to understand that the IT4IT standard is not a process model; it is complementary to process models. It is an information model based on the concept of an IT Value Chain and supported by the IT4IT Reference Architecture, a component model.
IT4IT is neutral with respect to development and delivery models. It is intended to support Agile as well as waterfall approaches, and Lean Kanban process approaches as well as fully elaborated IT service management process models.

1.2 Why Use the IT4IT Reference Architecture?

The following are key reasons to use IT4IT Reference Architecture standard:

- It provides a vendor-neutral, technology-agnostic, and industry-agnostic reference architecture for managing the business of IT, enabling insight for continuous improvement.
- It provides the capabilities for managing the business of IT that enable IT execution across the entire Value Chain in a better, faster, cheaper way with less risk.
- It is industry-independent to solve the same problems for everyone.

- It is designed for existing landscapes and accommodates future IT paradigms.

1.3 The Structure of the IT4IT Reference Architecture

The IT4IT standard consists of the following:

- A formal IT operating model based on a value chain approach known as the IT Value Chain (see Figure 1)
- A three-level functional reference architecture (see Figure 2) encompassing the four major IT value streams from the IT Value Chain.

What is a Value Chain?
A sequence of activities required to design, produce, and provide a specific good or service, and along which information, materials, and worth flows. See also Chapter 2.

1.3.1 The IT Value Chain

The IT4IT standard is organized around the IT Value Chain, with four value streams supported by a reference architecture to drive efficiency and agility.

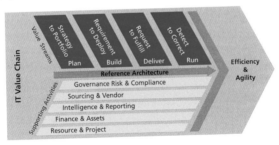

Figure 1: The IT Value Chain

The four value streams are:
- Strategy to Portfolio
- Requirement to Deploy
- Request to Fulfill
- Detect to Correct

Each IT Value Stream is centered on a key aspect of the service model, the essential data objects (information model), and functional components (functional model) that support it. Together, the four value streams play a vital role in helping IT control the service model as it advances through its lifecycle.

1.3.1.1 The Strategy to Portfolio (S2P) Value Stream

The **Strategy to Portfolio** (S2P) Value Stream places primary emphasis on controlling the business aspects of the service model (Conceptual Service). Here, demand for services (new or improved) from consumers is captured and the Conceptual Service Blueprint (data object/service model) created to represent the new or enhanced service. The Conceptual Service Blueprint is the bridge between business and IT in that it provides the business context for the service along with the high-level architectural attributes. For further detail see Chapter 3.

1.3.1.2 The Requirement to Deploy (R2D) Value Stream

The **Requirement to Deploy** (R2D) Value Stream consumes the Conceptual Service Blueprint and triggers service design work. This results in the creation (or modification) of the logical service model that contains more detailed requirements that describe more technical aspects of the service. The R2D Value Stream is where sourcing, development, builds, tests, and releases are created, resulting in a deployable service (expressed as the Service Release Blueprint data object). For further detail see Chapter 4.

1.3.1.3 The Request to Fulfill (R2F) Value Stream

The **Request to Fulfill** (R2F) Value Stream represents the point at which the consumer meets the provider. It is intended to enable a new, consumer-driven era in IT in that it exposes all available capabilities to consumers through an inviting service interface. Once the Logical Service Blueprint has been made available, service catalog entries (visible to service providers as a data object) can be created and shaped into consumable offers (visible to consumers as a data object). The R2F Value Stream initiates the activities associated both with creating a service instance in production run-time environments and those associated with fulfilling requests from individual consumers for services. For further details see Chapter 5.

1.3.1.4 The Detect to Correct (D2C) Value Stream

The **Detect to Correct** (D2C) Value Stream focuses on managing the availability and ongoing support of service execution. Once an instance of a service is "in production" the realized service model is expressed using detailed technical terms and represented as an aggregation of Configuration Items (CIs). Since services and service components are sourced from a mix of internal and external providers, holistic visibility of service model data and engagement with participants from across all value streams is essential for effective service management. For further details see Chapter 6.

1.3.2 The IT4IT Reference Architecture

The IT4IT Reference Architecture supports the IT Value Chain. It provides a prescriptive framework to support the value chain-based IT operating model and service-centric IT management ecosystem. It can be considered as describing the "IT for IT" (IT4IT) architecture and relationships.

A complete, detailed architecture for IT4IT would be unreadable, unmanageable, and impossible to understand. The solution is to use a layered refinement approach. Thus, the IT4IT Reference Architecture is communicated using multiple levels of abstraction. This decompositional approach is similar to that employed by other frameworks such as eTOM from the TM Forum. Each abstraction level expands on the prior to expose more details and prescriptive guidance.

There are five levels. The upper levels (1-3) are vendor-agnostic and provide more generic views that are suitable for strategy and planning purposes as well as for creating IT management product roadmaps. The lower levels (4-5) provide more specific details, ultimately arriving at implementation level or vendor-owned/controlled information. Content at these levels is suitable for developing implementation plans and for facilitating product design. The IT4IT Reference Architecture defines five abstraction levels as depicted in Figure 2.

Figure 2: IT4IT Reference Architecture Levels

The standard defines Levels 1 to 3. Levels 4 and 5 are not defined by the standard, which provides example guidance only at these levels. Product and service providers implement Levels 4 and 5.

The Level 1 Architecture is shown in Figure 3 which illustrates the focus on the entire IT Value Chain (for a description of the notation used see Chapter 2); everything from help desk, data centers, end user training, and hardware infrastructure to the administrators and technicians that keep everything running as part of its Requirements to Deploy or Detect to Correct value streams. Other value streams include Strategy to Portfolio (planning) and Request to Fulfill (consumption).

IT4IT Reference Architecture L1 V.2.0

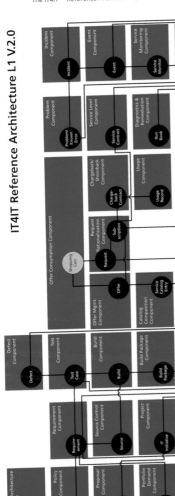

Figure 3: IT4IT Level 1 Reference Architecture Model

1.4 Positioning IT4IT

This section describes the positioning of the IT4IT Reference Architecture with respect to other Open Group standards and industry frameworks and methodologies.

1.4.1 The Need for an IT Reference Architecture

There are many standards related to IT and IT management. A careful analysis of the current landscape was carried out before the decision to develop yet another IT standard. What became apparent in the examination of the landscape was that there was indeed a gap where an IT reference architecture would fit. Mature industry verticals (e.g., retail, telecom) and professionalized management functions (e.g., finance, supply chain, HR) are evolving reference architectures, typically under some form of open consortium governance. Notable examples include:

- The work of the Association of Retail Technology Standards under the National Retail Federation (NRF/ARTS), including a comprehensive data model and process taxonomy. This data architecture is used extensively by vendors of retail technology as a standard for product interoperability.
- Frameworx, a suite of best practices and standards from the Tele-Management Forum (TM Forum). Frameworx and its related standards constitute a robust, multi-view architectural representation of telecom architecture, including processes, capabilities, data, and reference systems.

Other examples include:
- The ACORD Reference Architecture used in the insurance industry
- HR-XML of the HR Open Standards consortium
- The work of the Banking Industry Architecture Network (BIAN)
- The work of The Open Group Exploration, Mining, Metals, & Minerals (EMMM™) Forum

1.4.2 Relationship to TOGAF, ArchiMate, and ITIL

The IT4IT Reference Architecture can be related to TOGAF, ArchiMate, and ITIL as shown in Figure 4.

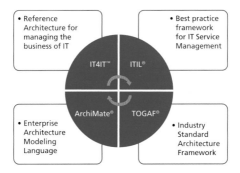

Figure 4: The Relationship to TOGAF, ArchiMate, and ITIL

1.4.2.1 The ArchiMate® Modeling Language

The IT4IT standard uses the ArchiMate notation to specify and publish the Reference Architecture and, hence, play back the use-cases for further improvement. The ArchiMate language (together with UML) is used at abstraction Level 3 as the primary method for communicating the IT4IT Reference Architecture specification.

1.4.2.2 ITIL®

ITIL is a best practice framework focused around processes, capabilities, and disciplines. The IT4IT standard embraces ITIL as guidance in the definition of the IT Value Chain-related capabilities and process-driven dependencies. The differences between IT4IT and ITIL are summarized in Appendix A.

1.4.2.3 The TOGAF® Framework

The TOGAF framework has been used to develop the IT4IT Reference Architecture: the IT4IT Value Streams and Reference Architecture thus include the EA capability. The benefit here is mutual: the evolution and use of the IT4IT standard – particularly around manageability and integration – will contribute to the extension and refinement of the TOGAF framework. The TOGAF methodology fits well with the "front end" or planning side of the IT Value Chain (S2P).

1.4.3 Relationship to Other Industry Frameworks and Methods

TOSCA, an OASIS standard, is an important emerging standard that plugs in at Level 3 (and lower) enabling specification and mapping of deployment structures from various sources.

COBIT – provides IT capability-related KPIs as guidance for IT4IT in the specification of key data artifacts.

SAFe – in general IT4IT is agnostic of the development methodology chosen, agile or waterfall; the reality is almost always a mix. More importantly, IT4IT is reflective and compliant with the enterprise planning levels and in-time planning methods based on queuing theory.

CMMI – applying IT4IT guidance and definition catalyzes organizational maturity, which can be expressed using the Capability Maturity Model Integration framework from Carnegie Mellon University. There is opportunity to leverage the CMMI process to define a specific IT4IT maturity level, and *vice versa*: to articulate IT4IT value stream achievements as measurable criteria associated with specific maturity levels.

Chapter 2
Basic IT4IT Concepts

This chapter describes the basic concepts of the IT4IT Reference Architecture.

This chapter includes:
- The IT Value Chain
- IT Value Streams

2.1 The IT Value Chain

A value chain is a series of activities that an organization performs in order to deliver something valuable, such as a product or service. Products pass through activities of a chain in order, and at each activity the product gains some value. A value chain framework helps organizations to identify the activities that are especially important for competitiveness – for the advancement of strategy and attainment of goals.

The IT Value Chain is grouped into two main categories of activities:
- Primary activities, which are concerned with the production or delivery of goods or services for which a business function, like IT, is directly accountable
- Supporting activities, which facilitate the efficiency and effectiveness of the primary activities

Value accrues through improvements in process efficiency and agility (as shown in Figure 1)[1].

---

1 For more on the value chain concept, see the referenced M. Porter: Competitive Advantage: Creating and Sustaining Superior Performance.

With services as the center of gravity, a value chain-based model for IT has been constructed by identifying the critical activities associated with the planning, sourcing, delivery, and management of services. The IT Value Chain content details the series of activities that every IT organization performs that add value to a business service or IT service. The IT4IT Reference Architecture breaks these activities down further to a Service Model and the essential functional components and data objects that IT produces or consumes in the IT Value Chain in order to advance the service lifecycle.

2.2 IT Value Streams

The IT4IT standard breaks down the IT Value Chain into four (4) value streams to help consumability and adoptability of the IT4IT Reference Architecture by IT organizations. Each value stream represents a key area of value that IT provides across the full service lifecycle.

The functional components in the IT Value Chain are grouped into four primary IT value streams and five supporting activities.

The four primary value streams are shown in Figure 5 and are as follows:
- Strategy to Portfolio
- Requirement to Deploy
- Request to Fulfill
- Detect to Correct

The primary value streams for the IT Value Chain generally align to what IT traditionally calls "Plan, Build, Deliver, Run". When used with an IT Value Chain-based model this is transformed into "Plan, Source, Offer, and Manage". These value streams are core to the IT function and have a vital role in helping to holistically run the full service lifecycle. These are usually hosted within IT.

Figure 5: Value Stream Overview

The five supporting activities (as shown in Figure 1) for the IT Value Chain are:

- Governance Risk & Compliance
- Sourcing & Vendor
- Intelligence & Reporting
- Finance & Assets
- Resource & Project

The supporting activities help ensure the efficiency and effectiveness of the IT Value Chain and primary value streams. These can be corporate or administrative functions that are hosted in the lines of business and/or IT.

2.3 The IT Value Chain and the IT4IT Reference Architecture

The IT Value Chain is the series of activities that IT performs to add value to a business service or IT service.

These activities are embodied in four value streams that provide a whole-of-life mapping for the business of IT, allowing executive managers to quickly engage in strategic and operational decision-making. The value streams, like the reference architecture, are process-agnostic, accommodating the full range of process models while maintaining overall cohesion and integrity.

The IT4IT Reference Architecture breaks down the activities in the IT Value Chain into four key pillars for IT:

1. The Service Model
2. The Information Model
3. The Functional Model
4. The Integration Model

Together these provide the prescription for the essential elements that IT must control to manage a service through its lifecycle.

Each IT Value Stream is centered on an essential element of the Service Model (see Section 2.3.1) and the configuration of key data objects (see Section 2.3.2, the Information Model), and functional components (see Section 2.3.3, the Functional Model) that support it.

2.3.1 The Service Model

Without a clear understanding of both the business and technology attributes of a service, there is no way to be certain that the desired outcome can be consistently attained and that the most optimal sourcing strategy will be applied. The Service Model construct in the architecture captures, connects, and maintains these service lifecycle attributes as the service progresses through its lifecycle.

Traditional IT lifecycles are oriented around projects, used to govern technology deployments. Therefore, the plan, build, run lifecycle is the stalwart for most IT organizations and very little data is captured and maintained for a service. The provider/broker model for the new style of IT places its focus on services as the primary IT deliverable and requires a higher degree of flexibility, velocity, and adaptability. A service-centric lifecycle framework is one that supports a continuous cycle of assessing the portfolio, sourcing and integrating components, and offering services to

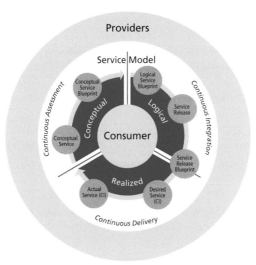

Figure 6: IT4IT Service Model

consumers. This requires greater degrees of control over the data associated with a service in its various stages.

The structure that binds the different abstraction levels of the Service Model together is called the "Service Model Backbone" (shown in Figure 6). The Service Model Backbone provides the data entities, attributes, and necessary relationships between them to ensure end-to-end traceability of a service from concept to instantiation and consumption. This means that using this data-driven, model-based approach will ensure that what is required is actually what gets delivered or, in other words, what is offered will produce the outcome that the consumer desires. Further, it allows the IT organization to effectively utilize a service-centric approach in creating and packaging its deliverables. This requires the creation of services from across resource and capability domains such as infrastructure, application components, database, middleware, monitoring, support, and so on. This enables the organization to improve their speed and consistency through higher re-use of pre-existing services and to embrace new technologies such as containers and micro-services in a more effective manner.

2.3.2 The Information Model

The Information Model comprises the set of service lifecycle data objects and their relationships.

It is important to understand the interactions between the processes that are executed to support IT and the underpinning systems that enable these processes, as well as the information that is exchanged between these systems as the process is run. The IT4IT standard adopts a novel perspective – that the Information Model and the systems (in terms of essential services that the components deliver) should be the basis for managing IT. This provides cohesion but without dictating process methods. Processes can evolve and be optimized and, depending on the situation, different processes or process models may be chosen and used.

The components and the data artifacts that they control and exchange must be highly dependable for effective IT management. That foundation is provided by the IT4IT Reference Architecture. Abstraction of the IT4IT Reference Architecture into process levels maintains conceptual cohesion and integrity but allows processes to be replaced, enabling IT organizations to make consistent long-term investment in IT management solutions. This also enables the IT organization to interact consistently with its suppliers and – even more importantly – enables the IT organization to gain deep and detailed insight into how well IT is performing and contributing to the business of which it is a part.

A similar "upwards" cohesion is enabled by the IT4IT standard. The four value streams provide a whole-of-life mapping for the business of IT. This perspective is similarly process-agnostic. Its derivation from the ubiquitous value chain makes it immediately familiar to executives and provides a similarly coherent basis for strategic and operational decision-making.

The IT4IT standard fills the persistent "vacuum" between strategy and governance frameworks and tools at the highest level and tool-specific architectural components at the operational level.

Each value stream produces and/or consumes data that together represents all of the information required to control the activities that advance a service through its lifecycle. This data has been referred to as "service lifecycle *data objects*" (data objects in short form). Some data objects contribute directly to creating and/or advancing the Service Model while others serve as connectors, providing the linkage between functional components and across value streams.

Data objects have the following characteristics:
- They describe an aspect of an IT service.
- They are inputs or outputs associated with an IT4IT functional component or a service lifecycle phase.
- They are uniquely identified, and have a lifecycle of their own.
- They maintain structured information that allows for relationship tracking and automation.

Service lifecycle data objects in the IT4IT Reference Architecture are grouped into two categories: *key* and *auxiliary*.

Data Object Type	Description	Symbol
Key Data Objects	Key data objects describe aspects of "how" services are created, delivered, and consumed; they are essential to managing the service lifecycle. Managing the end-to-end service lifecycle and associated measurement, reporting, and traceability would be virtually impossible without them. The IT4IT Reference Architecture defines 32 key data objects and most are depicted as black circles.	●
	Service models are a stand-alone subclass of key data objects that describe "what" IT delivers to its consumers. They represent the attributes of a service at three levels of abstraction: Conceptual, Logical, and Realized. These data objects are referred to as Service Model Backbone data objects (or service backbone data objects in short form) and depicted in this Pocket Guide using a light blue circle in the IT4IT Reference Architecture diagrams.	●
Auxiliary Data Objects	Auxiliary data objects provide context for the "why, when, where, etc." attributes and, while they are important to the IT function, they *do not play a vital role in managing the service lifecycle*. The IT4IT Reference Architecture currently describes eight (8) auxiliary data objects and they are depicted using a gray colored circle.	●

The essential relationships between data objects within and across value streams are defined in the IT4IT Reference Architecture and summarized in Chapter 3 through Chapter 6 of this Pocket Guide. These relationships function as a prescriptive guide for ensuring the integrity of the Service Model as it progresses through its lifecycle and facilitate traceability across value streams.

Relationships
The IT4IT Reference Architecture provides only the essential relationships and recognizes that there are other relationships that can exist but those are not part of the prescriptive guide.

Within the IT4IT Reference Architecture, the relationship between data objects is annotated as follows:

- 1 to 1 (1:1): implies that if there is a relationship, it is between two data objects. It does not imply that there will always be a relationship. For example, Events without Incidents or Incidents without Events are legitimate scenarios.
- 1 to many (1:n): implies that one data object relates (A) to one or more other data objects (B...) in scenarios where there is a relationship.
- Many to many (n:m): implies that both and A and B above can relate to zero, one, or many of the connected data objects.

Figure 7 provides an example of the relationship notation. The relationships and notation used here are for illustration purposes only and do not reflect the actual notation used or the relationship between the specific data objects shown.

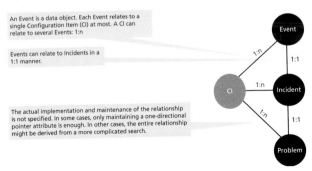

Figure 7: Data Objects and Relationships

Multiplicity Notation
In the IT4IT Reference Architecture notation, the multiplicity is always written horizontally (e.g., 1:1 in Figure 7). In some cases, the related entities are depicted vertically. When this occurs the general rules of mathematics should be applied to determine the relationship. This means the left position number/letter relates to the entity that is left or upward and the right position number/letter relates to the entity right or downward.

2.3.3 The Functional Model

The IT4IT Reference Architecture identifies and defines one of the essential building blocks – functional components – that create or consume data objects and can be aligned with the appropriate value streams. These functional components are based on real IT scenarios and use-cases.

The context for functional components starts with an IT "capability". A capability is the ability that an organization, person, or system possesses (function or activity it can perform) which produces an outcome of value through the utilization of a combination of people, process, methods, technology resources, and/or tools.

Functional components can be logically associated to IT capabilities for organizational clarity and underpinned with processes to drive uniformity and consistency.

A functional component is the smallest technology unit that can stand on its own and be useful as a whole to a customer. Functional components have defined input(s) and output(s) that are data objects and impact on a key data object (for example, a state change). Functional components typically control a single data object. A grouping of one or more functional components represents the technology elements of an IT capability.

Capturing the architecture in this manner and constructing the ecosystem using this approach delivers on the agility promise and ensures end-to-end traceability by focusing on data rather than process as the design guide. Processes can change, organizational structures can shift (such as centralized/decentralized), and yet the Information Model remains constant and the architectural integrity of the IT management ecosystem is not compromised.

2.3.3.1 Functional Component Overview

Functional components are grouped into two categories: *primary* and *secondary*. These are also referred to as "key" and "auxiliary", respectively.

Functional Component Type	Description	Symbol
Primary Functional Component	A primary (key) functional component is depicted using a blue colored rectangle and is core to a specific value stream. This means that the functional component plays a key role in the activities of a particular value stream. Without this functional component, the integrity of the data objects and thus the Service Model could not be maintained consistently and efficiently.	
Secondary Functional Component	Secondary (auxiliary) functional components are depicted in this Pocket Guide using a pale blue colored rectangle and represent some level of dependency or interaction with a value stream and its data objects. While they interact with a value stream, they are not core to it and are either primary to another value stream or supporting function or represent a capability.	

Notes

1. There a few conditions when a functional component is core to or co-owned by more than one value stream (e.g., the Change Control

functional component). When this occurs, the functional component is depicted using the blue colored rectangle in each value stream.

2. There is a unique condition in the R2F Value Stream where a relationship exists between functional components that is user experience-driven rather than data-driven. This condition is shown using an informal notation using a gray box with a black outline, as depicted in Figure 8.

Figure 8: Engagement Experience Portal Functional Component

The relationships and dependencies between data objects controlled by functional components are depicted using a solid line along with cardinality mapping. In addition to the entity relationships, functional components interact and exchange data to form the relationship. The data exchange between functional components is depicted using a dotted-line arrow to represent the direction of the flow.

Figure 9: Data Flows in the IT4IT Reference Architecture

2.3.4 The Integration Model

Integration between components in the traditional IT management ecosystem is based on capability and processes. The interfaces needed to accommodate the requirements associated with this approach are largely point-to-point between products to enable automation of inter-dependent workflows. Over time, this results in a complex web of connections that is virtually impossible to manage, making changes to any of the components a daunting task.

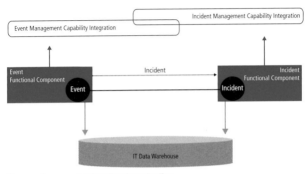

Figure 10: Engagement and Insight Information Flow

The IT4IT Reference Architecture defines an integration model with three types of integrations. These are used for simplifying the creation of an end-to-end IT management ecosystem using functional components. The three types are as follows:

- **System of record** integrations (data-centric integration, SoR in short form): These entity relationship definitions ensure the consistent management of the lifecycle for individual data objects, as well as ensuring that the data objects are consistently named and cross-linked through prescriptive data flows between functional components to maintain the integrity of the Service Model. They are represented by a dotted black line like the one in Figure 10.

- **System of engagement** integrations (experience-centric integration, SoE in short form): These are user interface integrations derived from value stream use-cases and user stories. These integrations deliver the technology underpinning for a capability by combining several functional components into a single user experience to facilitate human interaction with data objects. In the IT4IT Reference Architecture system of engagement integrations are represented by the blue arrow in Figure 10. In the actual notation, system of engagement integrations are depicted using a dotted blue line.

- **System of insight** integrations (intelligence, analytics, and KPI-centric integrations, SoI in short form): These are data-centric integrations driven by the need to provide traceability, end-to-end visibility, transparency, and to capture measurements related to services (for example, performance) or the service lifecycle (for example, fulfillment time). Further, these integrations can accommodate the exchange of both structured and unstructured data that is created across the value chain. System of insight integrations are represented by the gray arrow in Figure 10. The actual notation for system of insight integrations has not yet been defined as the architecture to support them will be developed in future releases. Therefore, while this integration is mentioned here, they do not appear in the current version documentation.

Chapter 3
The S2P Value Stream

This chapter describes the Strategy to Portfolio (S2P) Value Stream.

3.1 Overview

The Strategy to Portfolio (S2P) Value Stream:

- Provides the strategy to use to balance and broker your portfolio
- Provides a unified viewpoint across PMO, Enterprise Architecture, and service portfolio
- Improves data quality for decision-making
- Provides KPIs and roadmaps to improve business communication

The Strategy to Portfolio (S2P) Value Stream provides IT organizations with the optimal framework for interconnecting the different functions involved in managing the portfolio of services delivered to the enterprise. Activities such as capturing demand for IT services, prioritizing and forecasting investments, Service Portfolio Management, and Project Management require data consistency and transparency in order to maintain alignment between the business strategy and the IT portfolio.

Traditional IT planning and Portfolio Management activities put emphasis on capturing and tracking a collection of *projects* that represent the "orders" from the business for technology enablement. The S2P Value Stream places emphasis on the *service* and aims to provide a more holistic view of the IT portfolio to shape business investment decisions and connect IT costs with business value.

3.2 Key Value Propositions

The key value propositions for adopting the S2P Value Stream are as follows:

- Establish a holistic IT portfolio view across the IT PMO, and the Enterprise Architecture and Service Portfolio functional components so IT portfolio decisions are based on business priorities.
- Use well-defined system of records between the key areas that contribute to the IT Portfolio Management function to support consistent data for accurate visibility into business and IT demand.
- Endorse a Service Model that provides full service lifecycle tracking through conceptual, logical, and physical domains so it is possible to trace whether what was requested actually got delivered.

3.3 Activities

Typical activities include:

Strategy	Service Portfolio	Demand	Selection
• Define objectives • Align business and IT roadmaps • Set up standards and policies	• Enterprise architecture • Service portfolio rationalization • Create service blueprint and roadmap	• Consolidate demand • Analyze priority, urgency, and impact • Create new or tag existing demand	• Business value, risk, costs, benefits, & resources • What-if analysis • Ensure governance

Figure 11: Strategy to Portfolio Activities

The end-to-end IT portfolio view provided by the S2P Value Stream is accomplished by focusing on the service as the desired business outcome and exposing key data objects often unavailable using traditional planning methods. Defining the key data objects, the relationships between them, and their effect on the Service Models is core to the value stream approach. In addition, it provides inter-dependent functions such as Portfolio Demand, Enterprise Architecture, Service Portfolio, and Proposal functional components with data consistency and predefined data object exchanges in order to optimize the organization's IT Portfolio Management and service lifecycle management capability.

3.4 Value Stream Diagram

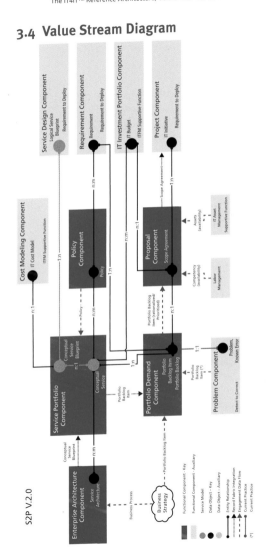

Figure 12: Strategy to Portfolio Level 2 Value Stream Diagram

3.5 Enterprise Architecture Functional Component

3.5.1 Purpose
The Enterprise Architecture functional component is in charge of the creation and management of long-term IT investment and execution plan-of-action that are critical to business strategic objectives.

3.5.2 Key Data Objects
The **Service Architecture** data object includes service blueprints, enterprise guiding principles, and technology roadmaps.

The key data attributes are ServiceID, ServiceComponent, ServiceDiagram.

3.5.3 Key Data Object Relationships
Service Architecture to Conceptual Service (n:m): Helps track which service components and service diagrams are allocated to which IT service(s).

3.5.4 Main Functions
The main functions of the Enterprise Architecture functional component are to:
- Identify strategic IT architectural components based on current business vision, strategy, goals, and requirements.
- Develop target state business, information, application, technology, and security blueprints based on strategies, principles, and policies.
- Develop IT roadmaps based on business roadmap and input.
- Develop and maintain enterprise guiding principles.
- Manage IT architecture guideline and standards.

Model

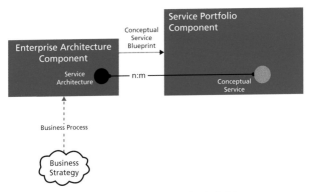

Figure 13: Enterprise Architecture Functional Component Level 2 Model

3.6 Policy Functional Component

3.6.1 Purpose

The Policy functional component manages creation, review, approval, and audit of all IT policies.

3.6.2 Key Data Objects

The **Policy** data object is a central repository for storing and organizing all types of IT policies based on various templates and classification criteria.

The key attributes are: PolicyID, PolicyDescription, ApplicableGeography.

3.6.3 Key Data Object Relationships

Policy to Conceptual Service (n:m): Multiple policies might be applicable for a single service or a single policy may be applicable for multiple services.

Policy to Requirement Functional Component (n:m): Requirements may be sourced from policies or may reference policies in order to remain in compliance with previously agreed policies for an organization.

3.6.4 Main Functions

The main functions of the Policy functional component are to:

- Align and map IT Policies to Service Architectures.
- Review and approve IT policies based on roles and responsibilities. It shall manage Policy distribution and acceptance based on predefined templates and schedules for designated IT stakeholders.
- Maintain complete Policy revision history, and review period or obsolescence rules set for all Policies.
- Optionally log and track IT Policy exceptions through an issue management mechanism. It may provide a consistent tracking feature for exception identification, evaluation, and status report leading to corrective action.
- Provide visibility into IT Policy attributes such as types, status, non-compliance, audit history, and issues.
- Manage overall IT governance Policies, and Policies applied to or associated with the particular services that may be managed downstream during service design.
- Manage IT security and regulatory Policies by incorporating external and internal security and regulatory compliances.
- Define pricing/costing Policies and capture information related to Service Contracts.

If a Service Portfolio functional component exists, the Policy functional component associates one or more policies to one or more Conceptual Services.

Model

Figure 14: Policy Functional Component Level 2 Model

3.7 Proposal Functional Component

3.7.1 Purpose

The Proposal functional component manages the portfolio of IT proposals that are proposed, approved, active, deferred, or rejected. This is the authoritative source for the list of IT proposals requested over a given time period that may result in the creation of Scope Agreements for projects. It can be used for building the IT investment plan of record for the company or a specific line of business or function.

3.7.2 Key Data Objects

The **Scope Agreement** data object reflects budget, cost/benefit projections, scope, and other key attributes of proposed work created from approved rationalized Portfolio Backlog Items.

The key attributes are: ScopeAgreementID, ScopeAgreementDescription, BusinessEntity.

3.7.3 Key Data Object Relationships

Scope Agreement to Portfolio Backlog Item (n:m): One Scope Agreement can be associated to one or more demand data objects.

Scope Agreement to IT Budget (n:1): This relationship helps track budget allocated to which Scope Agreement.

Scope Agreement to IT Initiative (1:n): This relationship helps track IT Initiative(s) to which Scope Agreement.

3.7.4 Main Functions

The main functions of the Proposal functional component are to:

- Create a Scope Agreement from rationalized Portfolio Backlog Items in the data object repository. A Scope Agreement can follow an expedited analysis and approval for high priority urgent items or agile development proposals. A Scope Agreement can also follow a structured analysis and approval via IT annual planning activities.
- Manage activities for Scope Agreements requiring an expedited analysis and approval:
  - Proposal created from a rationalized backlog item where the item requires high urgency due to business impact on an existing service.
  - Quickly evaluate the proposal and decide on the approval. If rejected, then notify the Portfolio Demand functional component.
  - Is there an existing IT Initiative that can be associated with the approved proposal? If yes, then create an updated Scope Agreement and update corresponding in-flight IT Initiative data object in the R2D Value Stream.
  - Create a new Scope Agreement. A new IT Initiative data object is created in the R2D Value Stream.
- Manage activities for proposals requiring structured analysis and approval:
  - Proposals are created from rationalized Portfolio Backlog Items in the Portfolio Backlog Item data object repository. Rationalized items are grouped based on priority and themes for a proposal creation purpose. Not all rationalized items will be grouped within proposals, as priority and cut-off must be decided.
  - Proposals are created periodically throughout the year or once a year during annual planning activities.

— Create a high-level labor consumption model for a proposal (for example, one project manager, five developers, and two QAs for the proposal). Validate labor consumption model against available internal and external labor pools.

— Create a high-level asset (non-labor) consumption model for a proposal. Validate asset consumption model against available internal and external assets (for example, traditional/private cloud/managed cloud/public cloud).

— Model ongoing labor and non-labor budget for annual and future operations.

— Define tangible and intangible benefits for each proposal. Tangible benefit may be cost savings or revenue growth, whereas intangible benefit may be strategic initiative support, competitive advantage, or compliance achieved. Work with a finance organization to validate tangible benefits. This can involve utilizing industry-specific methods of measuring the value of business processes and estimating the impact of the proposal on performance metrics.

— Ensure proposal meets the technology policies.

— Rank proposals based on benefits and risks, labor and non-labor consumption models, and ROI or other defined evaluation criteria.

— Build proposal portfolio scenarios using proposals, conduct "what if" analysis on the proposal scenarios, and approve the optimal proposal scenario and its proposals.

— Create resulting Scope Agreement(s). Retain Scope Agreement information to compare approved baseline and actual resulting benefits derived from completing the IT Initiatives.

• Review the Scope Agreement change request from the R2D Value Stream. The IT Initiative team working to deliver on the approved Scope Agreement may ask for change requests related to budget, resource, or timeline. Evaluate the change request and take action to update the existing Scope Agreement.

- The R2D Value Stream project portfolio is the authoritative source for the list of IT deliverables or services that will be rendered during a project lifecycle. The project portfolio views can be created for specific organizations like line of business portfolio or functions like financial views. The project portfolio is used for rationalizing and tracking resources across projects to best deliver on all projects. The project portfolio entries are actuated through a Project Management system. The project portfolio reports back to the investment portfolio in order to accurately track progress and outcomes for a given Scope Agreement.
- Identify security controls necessary for protecting the various classifications of data.

Model

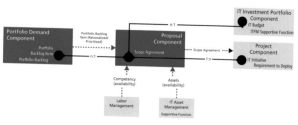

Figure 15: Proposal Functional Component Level 2 Model

3.8 Portfolio Demand Functional Component

3.8.1 Purpose

The Portfolio Demand functional component logs, maintains, and evaluates all demands (new service, enhancements, defects) coming into IT through a single funnel, correlating incoming demand to similar existing demand or creating new demand.

3.8.2 Key Data Objects

The **Portfolio Backlog Item** data object represents the repository of all incoming demands including but not limited to new requests, enhancement requests, and defect fix requests.

The key attributes are: DemandID, DemandDescription, Source, ITServiceID, DemandFulfillmentStatus, DecisionMaker.

3.8.3 Key Data Object Relationships

Portfolio Backlog Item to Conceptual Service (n:1): One Conceptual Service may be related to one or more Portfolio Backlog Items.

Portfolio Backlog Item to Requirement (1:n): A Portfolio Backlog Item is mapped to one or more Requirements that will need to be delivered to successfully fulfill the demand.

Portfolio Backlog Item to Scope Agreement (n:1): One or more Portfolio Backlog Items may be included in a Scope Agreement.

3.8.4 Main Functions

The main functions of the Portfolio Demand functional component are to:
- Capture Portfolio Backlog Items from business.
- Capture Portfolio Backlog Items from Problem Management activities.
- Capture Portfolio Backlog Items from the Service Portfolio functional component activities.

If a Proposal functional component exists, then the Portfolio Demand functional component categorizes and groups the demands and then pushes the demands to the Proposal functional component.

If a Requirement functional component exists, the Portfolio Demand functional component associates one or more Requirements (user stories, use-cases, business rules, etc.) to a Portfolio Backlog Item.

The Portfolio Demand functional component may support backlog item data object backlog ranking, trending, and analysis based on requested services, timeline, business unit origination, etc.

Model

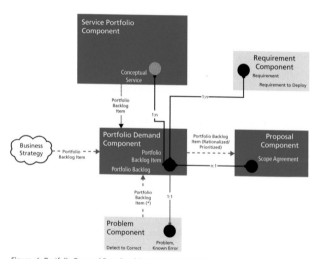

Figure 16: Portfolio Demand Functional Component Level 2 Model

3.9 Service Portfolio Functional Component

3.9.1 Purpose

The purpose of the Service Portfolio functional component is to manage the portfolio of services in plan, transition, production, and retirement.

It is the authoritative source for the list of services that IT delivers, has delivered in the past, or brokers to itself and business. Any IT service within the Service Portfolio functional component often corresponds to one or more entries in the Offer Catalog.

3.9.2 Key Data Objects

The **Conceptual Service** (data object): The Service Model is an authoritative source for the list of services that the enterprise consumes. It represents services planned, in transition, in production, or retired.

The key attributes are: ServiceID, ConceptualServiceDetails, ServiceOwner, ServiceStatus.

The **Conceptual Service Blueprint** (data object) contains the list of all service blueprints associated with a given Conceptual Service. (Each Conceptual Service Blueprint has a comprehensive view of the service that depicts endpoints and interfaces that can be understood by Architects and BRMs.)

The key attributes are: ConceptualServiceBlueprintID, ConceptualServiceBlueprint, ServiceID.

3.9.3 Key Data Object Relationships

Conceptual Service data object:

- **Service Architecture to Conceptual Service** (n:m): Traceability is maintained between one or more Conceptual Services and the Enterprise Architecture drawings, diagrams, and other documents that describe those services.
- **Conceptual Service to Portfolio Backlog Item** (1:n): One Conceptual Service may be related to one or more Portfolio Backlog Items.
- **Conceptual Service to IT Budget** (n:m): Budget for one Conceptual Service may be spread across multiple budget items and one budget item could hold budget for multiple Conceptual Services.

- **Conceptual Service to Policy** (n:m): Multiple Policies might be applicable for a single service or a single Policy may be applicable for multiple services.

Conceptual Service Blueprint data object:
- **Conceptual Service to Conceptual Service Blueprint** (1:n): One Conceptual Service may have multiple Conceptual Service Blueprints.
- **IT Cost Model to Conceptual Service Blueprint** (1:n): One IT cost model (rule engine) can be applicable for multiple Conceptual Service Blueprints.
- **Conceptual Service Blueprint to Logical Service Blueprint** (1:n): One Conceptual Service Blueprint could have one or more Logical Service Blueprints.

3.9.4 Main Functions

The main functions of the Service Portfolio functional component are to:
- Assess the effectiveness and efficiency of current services delivered to business.
- Manage all inventory information about services or applications; including business benefits, risk, quality, fitness-for-purpose, etc.
- Compare similar services or applications to identify rationalization opportunities.
- Evaluate the portfolio with regard to value/cost performance and risk/ criticality. These methods are used to maximize portfolio value, align and prioritize resource allocations, and balance supply and demand.
- Review proposed portfolio changes; decide whether to keep, retire, or modernize services or applications.
- Create, review, and update service roadmaps.
- Determine and track service budgets/actuals information.
- Create and maintain service blueprints and endpoints. A service blueprint is a set of service endpoints that support business processes. A service blueprint provides service process and delivery visualization

Model

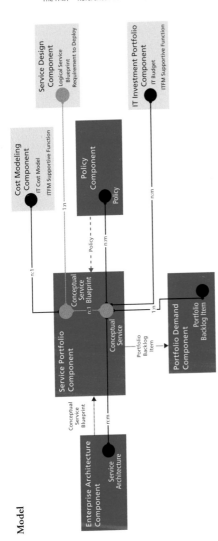

Figure 17: Service Portfolio Functional Component Level 2 Model

from the customer's point of view. A service blueprint also maintains traceability of Logical and Physical (realized) Service Models.

If a Portfolio Backlog Item exists, the Service Portfolio functional component associates a Conceptual Service to one or more Portfolio Backlog Items.

If a Policy exists, the Service Portfolio functional component should comply with one or more applicable Policies.

3.10 IT Investment Portfolio Auxiliary Functional Component

3.10.1 Purpose

The IT Investment Portfolio Auxiliary functional component is auxiliary to the S2P Value Stream and is primary in the IT Financial Management guidance document. Its main purpose includes managing the authoritative list of all IT investments, facilitating forecasting and budgeting activities, providing guidelines and information (e.g., unit costs) to be followed while estimating costs of proposed IT Initiatives, and establishing common governance and control mechanisms for approval/rejections of any proposed IT Initiatives.

3.10.2 Key Data Objects

The **IT Budget** data object is an authoritative list of approved IT investment pertaining to a proposed scope of work. This set of records can be used to identify approved budget over different time periods; e.g., by financial year.

The key attributes are: FinancialPeriod, ServiceID, ScopeAgreementID, BudgetType, RequestedBudget, ApprovedBudget, Spend.

Model

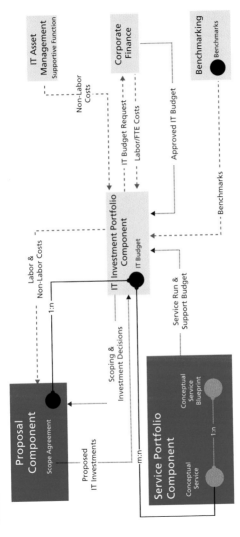

Figure 18: IT Investment Portfolio Auxiliary Functional Component Level 2 Model

3.10.3 Key Data Object Relationships

IT Budget to Conceptual Service (n:m): This relationship helps track how much IT Budget is allocated to which IT service(s).

IT Budget to Scope Agreement (1:n): This relationship helps track how much IT Budget is allocated to which Scope Agreement(s).

3.10.4 Main Functions

The main functions of the IT Investment Portfolio functional component are to:

- Be the system of records for all IT investments.
- Manage the entire IT investment lifecycle.
- Provide labor and non-labor cost estimates and other guidelines to the Proposal functional component.

Various proposal managers working on their respective proposals should send the information on proposed IT investments to the IT Investment Portfolio functional component, which manages them as follows:

- Accept inputs from the Service Portfolio functional component to include OpEx (Operating Expenditure) budget requests for keeping live services operational.
- Route these proposals/budget requests for necessary approvals with the respective governing committee.
- Communicate the status of the final investment decisions back to the respective stakeholders.

Chapter 4
The R2D Value Stream

This chapter describes the Requirement to Deploy (R2D) Value Stream.

4.1 Overview

The Requirement to Deploy (R2D) Value Stream:

- Provides a framework for creating, modifying, or sourcing a service
- Supports agile and traditional development methodologies
- Enables visibility of the quality, utility, schedule, and cost of the services you deliver
- Defines continuous integration and deployment control points

The Requirement to Deploy (R2D) Value Stream provides the framework for creating/sourcing new services or modifying those that already exist. The goal of the R2D Value Stream is to ensure predictable, cost-effective, high quality results. It promotes high levels of re-use and the flexibility to support multi-sourcing. The R2D Value Stream is process-agnostic in that, while methods and processes may change, the functional components and data objects that comprise the value stream remain constant. Therefore, it is complementary to both traditional and new methods of service development like agile, SCRUM, or DevOps.

The R2D Value Stream consumes the Conceptual Service Blueprint produced in the S2P Value Stream and through a series of design, development, and testing functions enables the development of the Logical Service Model for the service. The Logical Service Model is elaborated on until it represents a release that can be commissioned into a production state using standard deployment methods or in an on-demand manner using a user-driven catalog experience. Once deployed into a production state, the Physical Service Model is generated that is comprised of the physical elements that comprise the service.

4.2 Key Value Propositions

The key value propositions for adopting the R2D Value Stream are:

- Ensure that the Service Release meets business expectations (quality, utility).
- Make service delivery predictable, even across globally dispersed teams and suppliers, and multiple development methodologies while preserving innovation.
- Standardize service development and delivery to the point where re-use of service components is the norm.
- Build a culture of collaboration between IT operations and development to improve Service Release success.

4.3 Activities

Typical activities include:

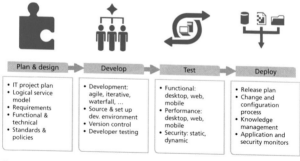

Figure 19: Requirement to Deploy Activities

4.4 Value Stream Diagram

R2D V.2.0

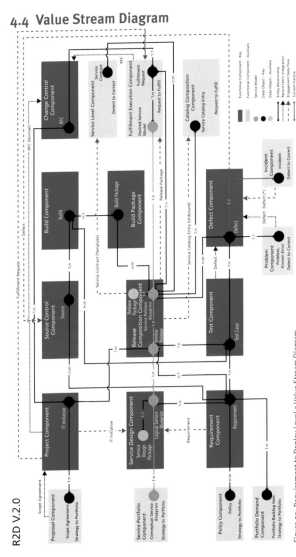

Figure 20: Requirement to Deploy Level 2 Value Stream Diagram

4.5 Project Functional Component

4.5.1 Purpose

The Project functional component coordinates the creation and provides ongoing execution oversight of IT Initiatives aimed at the creation of new or enhancements to existing services. The IT Initiatives are based on the specifications outlined in the Scope Agreement.

The Project functional component will govern, coordinate, influence, and direct initiative execution. It will ensure financial goals and boundary conditions are adhered to and coordinate the acquisition of resources (hardware, software, and people) required to source/create a service in a particular project.

4.5.2 Key Data Objects

The **IT Initiative** data object details the scope of the work to be performed and created from and associated with the Scope Agreement.

The key attributes are: ITInitiativeID, ITInitiativeName, ITInitiativeStatus, ServiceReleaseID, RFCID, ScopeAgreementID.

4.5.3 Key Data Object Relationships

Scope Agreement to IT Initiative (1:n): Maintain a linkage between the proposal, which authorized one or more IT Initiatives.

IT Initiative to Service Release (1:n): An IT Initiative will manage the creation of one or more Service Releases required to deliver the IT Initiative.

IT Initiative to Request for Change (RFC) (1:n): An Initiative will be related to one or many RFC records in order to manage all changes resulting from a single work effort (initiative).

4.5.4 Main Functions

The main functions of the Project functional component are to:

- Be the system of record (authoritative source) for all IT Initiatives.
- Manage the lifecycle of the IT Initiative.
- Manage the status of the IT Initiative.
- Allow recursive relationships between IT Initiatives.
- Associate an IT Initiative to a service.
- Optionally associate an IT Initiative with IT budget in the IT Financial Management supporting function.

If a Change Control functional component exists, the Project functional component associates an IT Initiative to one or more RFCs, and can submit one or more RFCs required for the IT Initiative.

If a Fulfillment Execution functional component exists, the Project functional component can manage the Fulfillment Request data flow to the Fulfillment Execution functional component, and can send a request to the Fulfillment Execution functional component when resources are required for the IT Initiative.

If a Proposal functional component exists, the Project functional component associates a Scope Agreement to one or more IT Initiatives, and is able to receive the Scope Agreement from the Proposal functional component.

If a Service Design functional component exists, the Project functional component can provide IT Initiative information required for Service Design to the Service Design functional component.

Model

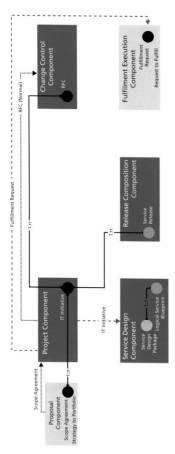

Figure 21: Project Functional Component Level 2 Model

4.6 Requirement Functional Component

4.6.1 Purpose

The Requirement functional component manages requirements through the lifecycle of a service. It collects, refines, scopes, and tracks progress of Requirements even before and after an IT Initiative has concluded. It maintains the traceability of each Requirement to the original source (demand, IT or business standard or policy, and/or requestor) and to appropriate source and/or test cases throughout the service lifecycle.

4.6.2 Key Data Objects

The **Requirement** data object records details of the needs or conditions to meet for a new or altered service.

The key attributes are: RequirementID, RequirementType, RequirementSummary, LogicalServiceBlueprintID, PolicyID, PortfolioBacklogID, ServiceReleaseID, SourceID, TestCaseID.

4.6.3 Key Data Object Relationships

Logical Service Blueprint to Requirement (1:n): The Logical Service Blueprint is the Service Design which fulfills one or more Requirements.

Service Release to Requirement (1:n): The Service Release delivers a service which fulfills one or more Requirements.

Requirement to Test Case (1:n): A Requirement is traced to one or more Test Cases to ensure stated needs or conditions have been successfully delivered or met.

Portfolio Backlog Item to Requirement (1:n): A Portfolio Backlog Item is mapped to one or more Requirements that will need to be delivered to successfully fulfill the demand.

Policy to Requirement (n:m): Requirements may be sourced from policies or may reference policies in order to remain in compliance to previously agreed policies for an organization.

4.6.4 Main Functions

The main functions of the Requirement functional component are to:
- Be the system of record (authoritative source) for all Requirements.
- Manage the lifecycle of the Requirement.
- Manage the state of a Requirement.
- Allow recursive relationships between Requirements.
- Allow hierarchical relationships between Requirements.
- Associate a requirement to a service.

If a Portfolio Demand functional component exists, the Requirement functional component associates one or more Requirements to a Portfolio Backlog Item from which these Requirements originate.

If a Service Design functional component exists, the Requirement functional component can manage the data flow to provide Requirement information to the Service Design functional component and can associate one or more Requirements to a single Logical Service Model.

If a Release Composition functional component exists, the Requirement functional component associates one or more Requirements to a Service Release that will fulfill these Requirements.

If a Test functional component exists, the Requirement functional component allows a Requirement to be traced to one or more Test Cases designed to test this Requirement.

If a Policy functional component exists, the Requirement functional component allows one or more Requirements to be associated to one or more policies from which these Requirements originate.

If a Source data object exists, the Requirement functional component
allows one or more Requirements to be traced to one or more Sources.

Model

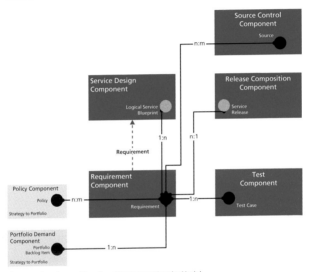

Figure 22: Requirement Functional Component Level 2 Model

4.7 Service Design Functional Component

4.7.1 Purpose

The Service Design functional component identifies the new or existing
services required to meet the needs of the Scope Agreement and IT
Initiative, including both service systems and service offers. Based on the
Conceptual Service Blueprint and Portfolio Backlog Items, it produces a
Logical Service Blueprint that describes the service structure and behavior
considering both the service system and the service offer.

It creates a service design specification document (Service Design Package) that is compliant with all standards and policies, that meet functional and non-functional requirements and that is consistent with Enterprise Architecture principles and requirements.

4.7.2 Key Data Objects

The **Logical Service Blueprint** data object represents the logical design of the service based on the Requirements and Conceptual Service Blueprint.

The key attributes are: LogicalServiceBlueprintID, LogicalServiceBlueprintVersion, ServiceDesignPackageID, ServiceDesignPackageVersion, ConceptualServiceBlueprintID, RequirementID, ServiceRealeaseID.

4.7.3 Key Data Object Relationships

Conceptual Service Blueprint to Logical Service Blueprint (1:n): The Conceptual Service Blueprint represents the high-level design of a service or changes to a service and leads to the creation of one or many Logical Service Blueprints.

Logical Service Blueprint to Requirement (1:n): The Logical Service Blueprint is the service design that fulfills one or more Requirements.

Logical Service Blueprint to Service Release (1:n): A Logical Service Blueprint can lead to the creation of one or more Service Releases.

4.7.4 Main Functions

The Service Design functional component is the system of record (authoritative source) for all Logical Service Blueprints. It associates a Logical Service Blueprint to a service. It can also associate a Logical Service Blueprint to a Service Design Package.

If a Service Portfolio functional component exists, the Service Design functional component associates one or more Logical Service Blueprints to a Conceptual Service Blueprint, and can receive the Conceptual Service specification and design several Logical Service Blueprints that represent it.

If a Project functional component exists, the Service Design functional component can receive IT Initiative information, which includes the scope and some content based on which the service is designed.

If a Requirement functional component exists, the Service Design functional component associates one or more Requirements to the Logical Service Blueprint, and can receive Requirement information from the Requirement functional component used to design the Logical Service Blueprint and create design specifications.

If a Release Composition functional component exists, the Service Design functional component associates a Logical Service Blueprint to one or more Service Releases which are detailed and designed to deliver the Logical Service Blueprint.

Model

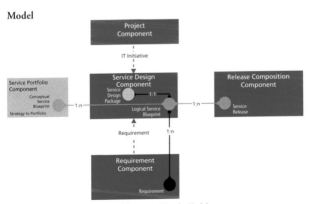

Figure 23: Service Design Functional Component Level 2 Model

4.8 Source Control Functional Component

4.8.1 Purpose

The Source Control functional component manages the development of source code or infrastructure based on the Logical Service Blueprint, Service Design Package, and IT Initiative priorities. It ensures that the source code meets the design specifications, organizational policies, standards, and non-functional requirements so that the service can be operated successfully and meets customer expectations.

It manages source code images and stores them in a Source data object repository and delivers the Source data object to the Build functional component. It also receives Defects and input from the Defect functional component to enable the development of fixes or documented workarounds.

4.8.2 Key Data Objects

The **Source** data object is the created or purchased solution to meet the requirements for a particular Service Release.

The key attributes are: SourceID, SourceVersion, BuildID, RequirementID.

 Source does not always equal "source code". Consider all use-cases such as "source code" for services produced on-premise, to contracts or entitlements for services simply subscribed to, to the purchase and implementation of a Commercial Off-The-Shelf (COTS) application.

4.8.3 Key Data Object Relationships

Source to Requirement (n:m): Source will fulfill one or many Requirements, and for a given Service Release, there could be multiple Sources created/modified.

Source to Build (1:n): Source can create one or many Builds.

4.8.4 Main Functions

The main functions of the Source Control functional component are to:

- Be the system of record (authoritative source) for all Source.
- Manage the lifecycle of the Source.
- Allow recursive relationships between Source.
- Allow hierarchical relationships between Source.
- Associate Source to a service.

If a Requirement functional component exists, the Source Control functional component associates one or many Requirements to one or many Sources, which includes the content that fulfills these Requirements.

If a Build functional component exists, the Source Control functional component associates one or many Builds to the related Source.

If a Defect functional component exists, the Source Control functional component can receive Defect information from the Defect functional component so Defects can be fixed in future versions of that Source.

Model

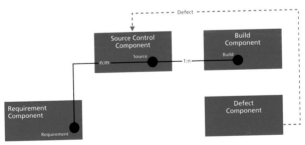

Figure 24: Source Control Functional Component Level 2 Model

4.9 Build Functional Component

4.9.1 Purpose

The Build functional component receives the Source data object from the Source Control functional component and manages the creation, implementation, automation, and security and storage of all Builds. It manages Builds and versioning in a Definitive Media Library (DML).

It automates the Build process through automated Build storage procedures and automated compilation techniques and tools. It also runs dynamic application security testing.

4.9.2 Key Data Objects

The **Build** data object is created from Source and versioned.

The key attributes are: BuildID, BuildVersion, SourceID, TestCaseID, BuildPackageID.

4.9.3 Key Data Object Relationships

Source to Build (1:n): Source can be built multiple times to create several Build versions.

Build to Test Case (n:m): One or many Builds can be related to one or many Test Cases used as part of the Build creation.

Build Package to Build (1:n): A Build Package is comprised of one or many Builds.

4.9.4 Main Functions

The main functions of the Build functional component are to:
• Be the system of record (authoritative source) for all Builds.

- Manage the version of each individual Build.
- Associate a Build to a service.

If a Source Control functional component exists, the Build functional component associates Source to one or many Builds.

If a Test functional component exists, the Build functional component associates one or many Builds to one or many Test Cases that are executed as part of the Build creation.

If a Build Package functional component exists, the Build functional component associates one or many Builds to a Build Package.

Model

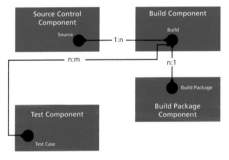

Figure 25: Build Functional Component Level 2 Model

4.10 Build Package Functional Component

4.10.1 Purpose

Creation of a deployable package made up of one or many Builds. Manage the Build Packages and relationships to the Service Release Blueprints.

4.10.2 Key Data Objects

The **Build Package** data object is a compilation of one or many Builds in a deployable package.

The key attributes are: BuildPackageID, BuildID, ServiceReleaseBlueprintID.

4.10.3 Key Data Object Relationships

Build Package to Build (1:n): The Build Package is comprised of one or more Builds.

Build Package to Service Release Blueprint (n:m): One or more Build Packages can be associated to one or more Service Release Blueprints.

4.10.4 Main Functions

The main functions of the Build Package functional component are to:

- Be the system of record (authoritative source) for all Build Packages.
- Associate a Build Package to a service.

Model

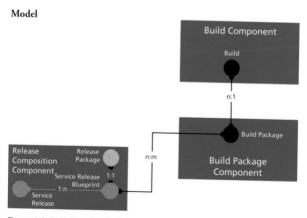

Figure 26: Build Package Functional Component Level 2 Model

If a Build functional component exists, the Build Package functional component associates one or more Builds to a Build Package.

If a Release Composition functional component exists, the Build Package functional component associates one or more Service Release Blueprints to one or more Build Packages.

4.11 Release Composition Functional Component

4.11.1 Purpose
The Release Composition functional component creates the Release Package, Service Release, Service Release Blueprints, and overall Service Release for developing and delivering new or changed services to the R2F Value Stream Fulfillment Execution functional component to facilitate a smooth transition to IT operations.

It manages the release artifacts within the Release Package by centralizing all elements of the Service Release Blueprint from the various functional components and begins the creation of monitors, batch processing, backup/restore, etc. for the service, to ensure supportability as part of IT operations enablement.

4.11.2 Key Data Objects
The **Service Release** (data object) represents the release of a given service.

The key attributes are: ServiceReleaseID, LogicalServiceBlueprintID, ITInitiativeID, ServiceReleaseBlueprintID, RequirementID, TestCaseID.

The **Service Release Blueprint** (data object) contains the information and details related to a specific release to a specific environment.

The key attributes are: ServiceReleaseBlueptintID, ServiceReleaseBlueprintDescription, MasterServiceID, ServiceReleaseID, BuildPackageID, DesiredServiceModelID, FulfillmentID, ServiceContractID, ServiceID, DefectID.

4.11.3 Key Data Object Relationships

The Service Release data object:

- **Logical Service Blueprint to Service Release** (1:n): A Logical Service Blueprint can lead to the creation of one or more Service Releases.
- **IT Initiative to Service Release** (1:n): An IT Initiative will manage the creation of one or more Service Releases defined to deliver the content of the IT Initiative.
- **Service Release to Service Release Blueprint** (1:n): A Service Release can be released to multiple environments based on the associated Service Release Blueprints.
- **Service Release to Requirement** (1:n): The Service Release delivers a service which fulfills one or more Requirements.
- **Service Release to Test Case** (1:n): A Service Release can be validated by one or many Test Cases/

The Service Release Blueprint data object:

- **Service Release to Service Release Blueprint** (1:n): A Service Release can be released to multiple environments based on the associated Service Release Blueprints.
- **Service Release Blueprint to Build Package** (n:m): One or more Build Packages can be associated to one or more Service Release Blueprints.
- **Service Release Blueprint to Desired Service Model** (1:n): One Service Release Blueprint can be translated to one or more Desired Service Models.
- **Service Release Blueprint to Fulfillment Request** (1:n): One Service Release Blueprint is used for service instantiation by one or many Fulfillment Requests.

- **Service Release Blueprint to Service Contract** (n:m): One or more Service Release Blueprints contain the template of one or more Service Contracts.
- **Service Catalog Entry to Service Release Blueprint** (1:n): Each Service Catalog Entry is created based on definitions of a Service Release Blueprint.
- **Service Release Blueprint to Defect** (n:m): One or more Service Release Blueprints can contain one or may Defects in the form of Problems/Known Errors.

4.11.4 Main Functions

The main functions of the Release Composition functional component are to:

- Be the system of record (authoritative source) for all Service Releases.
- Associate a Service Release to a service.
- Allow a recursive relationship between Service Releases.
- Associate a Service Release to one or more Service Release Blueprints.
- Be the system of record for all Service Release Blueprints.
- Associate a Service Release Blueprint to a service.
- Associate a Service Release Blueprint to a Release Package.

If a Project functional component exists, the Release Composition functional component associates one IT Initiative to one or more Service Releases that are defined to deliver this IT Initiative.

If a Service Design functional component exists, the Release Composition functional component associates one Logical Service Blueprint to one or more Service Releases that are designed to deliver this Logical Service.

If a Requirement functional component exists, the Release Composition functional component associates one Service Release with one or more Requirements that are fulfilled in this release.

If a Test functional component exists, the Release Composition functional component associates one Service Release with one or more Test Cases, and can receive test-related information that should be included in the Release Package from Test Management.

If a Build Package functional component exists, the Release Composition functional component associates one or more Service Release Blueprints to one or more Build Packages, and can receive one or more Build Packages that should be included in the Service Release Blueprint.

If a Service Level functional component exists, the Release Composition functional component can provide service contract information for creating a Service Contract, and associate one or more Service Release Blueprints to one or more Service Contracts.

If a Fulfillment Execution functional component exists, the Release Composition functional component can provide information required for service instantiation to the Fulfillment Execution functional component, associate a Service Release Blueprint to one or more Desired Service Models, and associate a Service Release Blueprint to one or more Fulfillment Requests.

If a Catalog Composition functional component exists, the Release Composition functional component can provide information required for creating a Service Catalog Entry to the Catalog Composition functional component, and associate a Service Release Blueprint to one or more Service Catalog Entry(ies).

If a Defect functional component exists, the Release Composition functional component associates one or more Service Release Blueprints to one or more Defects, and can receive Defect-related information that should be included in the Release Package.

Model

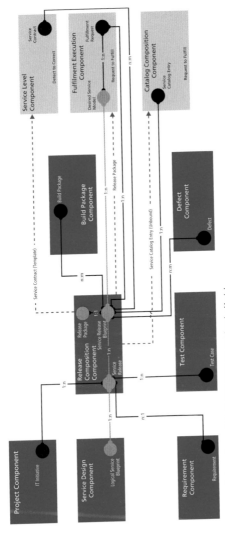

Figure 27: Release Composition Functional Component Level 2 Model

4.12 Test Functional Component

4.12.1 Purpose

The Test functional component plans and executes tests that ensure the IT service will support the customer's requirements at the agreed service levels. It prepares test environment, plans and designs tests, and executes all functional and non-functional tests including performance and stress testing.

It creates Defect data objects that are consumed by the Defect functional component. It provides test execution reports for the tested Requirements and ensures that the operations tooling works as expected (monitors, etc.).

4.12.2 Key Data Objects

The **Test Case** data object is used to validate that the Service Release is fit-for-purpose.

The key attributes are: TestCaseID, TestCaseSummary, TestCaseStatus, ServiceReleaseID, BuildID, RequirementID, DefectID.

4.12.3 Key Data Object Relationships

Requirement to Test Case (1:n): A Requirement is associated to one or more Test Cases that validates this Requirement.

Service Release to Test Case (1:n): A Service Release is associated to one or more Test Cases which are executed as part of this Service Release.

Test Case to Build (n:m): One or more Test Cases can be associated with one or more Builds that uses this Test Case as part of the Build creation.

Test Case to Defect (1:n): One Test Case can be associated to one or more Defects that are reported as a result of this test.

4.12.4 Main Functions

The main functions of the Test functional component are to:

- Be the system of record (authoritative source) for all Test Cases.
- Manage the lifecycle of the Test Case.
- Allow recursive relationships between Test Cases.
- Associate a Test Case to a service.

If a Build functional component exists, the Test functional component associates one or more Test Cases to one or more Builds that uses this Test Case as part of the Build creation.

If a Requirement functional component exists, the Test functional component associates a Requirement to one or more Test Cases that validates this Requirement.

If a Defect functional component exists, the Test functional component associates a Test Case to one or more Defects that result from this test and provides Defect information to the Defect functional component.

Model

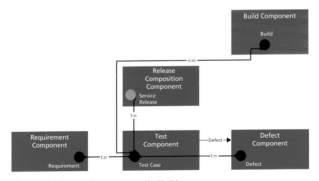

Figure 28: Test Functional Component Level 2 Model

4.13 Defect Functional Component

4.13.1 Purpose

The Defect functional component keeps track of all Defects by registering Defects of all types (including security-related Defects). It analyzes Defects and finds resolutions. It also associates Defects with Requirements.

It documents issues that should be communicated to the Release Composition functional component. It decides on target release and reports Defect status. It also converts Defects not resolved to Known Errors for Problem Management.

4.13.2 Key Data Objects

The **Defect** data object is an issue with the Service Release Blueprint which should be remediated to fulfill the associated Requirements.

The key attributes are: DefectID, DefectDescription, DefectStatus, ServiceReleaseBlueprintID, TestCaseID, KnownErrorID.

4.13.3 Key Data Object Relationships

Test Case to Defect (1:n): One Test Case can be associated to one or more Defects that results from the test.

Defect to Service Release Blueprint (n:m): One or more Service Release Blueprints are associated to one or more Defects which are included in the Release Package as Problems/Known Errors.

Known Error to Defect (1:1): A Known Error is associated to a Defect when the Known Error is found to be a Defect.

4.13.4 Main Functions

The main functions of the Defect functional component are to:

- Be the system of record (authoritative source) for all Defects.
- Manage the lifecycle of the Defect.
- Associate a Defect to a service.

If a Release Composition functional component exists, the Defect functional component associates one or more Service Release Blueprints to one or more Defects, which reflects Defects that should be published as Problems/Known Errors.

If a Source Control functional component exists, the Defect functional component can provide Defect information to the Source Control functional component.

If a Test functional component exists, the Defect functional component receives Defect information from the Test functional component, and associates a Test Case to one or more Defects.

If a Problem functional component exists, the Defect functional component associates a Known Error to a Defect and receives Defect information from a Known Error.

Model

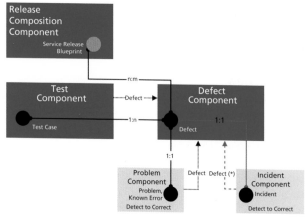

Figure 29: Defect Functional Component Level 2 Model

Chapter 5
The R2F Value Stream

This chapter describes the Request to Fulfill (R2F) Value Stream.

5.1 Overview

The Request to Fulfill (R2F) Value Stream:

- Helps your IT organization transition to a service broker model
- Presents a single catalog with items from multiple supplier catalogs
- Efficiently manages subscriptions and total cost of service
- Manages and measures fulfillments across multiple suppliers

The Request to Fulfill (R2F) Value Stream is a framework connecting the various consumers (business users, IT practitioners, or end customers) with goods and services that are used to satisfy productivity and innovation needs. The R2F Value Stream places emphasis on time-to-value, repeatability, and consistency for consumers looking to request and obtain services from IT. The R2F Value Stream helps IT optimize both service consumption and fulfillment experiences for users by delineating functions for an Offer Catalog and Catalog Composition. The R2F Value Stream framework provides a single consumption experience to consumers for seamless subscription to both internal and external services, as well as managing subscriptions and routing fulfillments to different service providers using the R2F Value Stream framework.

The R2F Value Stream plays an important role in helping IT organizations transition to a service broker model. Enterprise customers have been using external suppliers for goods and services for many years. The IT multi-sourcing environment will accelerate as companies adopt cloud computing offerings like Infrastructure as a Service (IaaS), Platform as a Service (PaaS), and Software as a Service (SaaS).

5.2 Key Value Propositions

The key value propositions for adopting the R2F Value Stream are:

- Provide a portal and catalog blueprint for facilitating a service consumption experience that allows consumers to easily find and subscribe to services through self-service, regardless of sourcing approach.
- Establish the model for moving from traditional IT request management to service brokerage.
- Increase fulfillment efficiency through standard change deployment and automation.
- Leverage the common Service Model to reduce custom service request fulfillments and design automated fulfillments.
- Facilitate a holistic view and traceability across service subscription, service usage, and service chargeback as applicable.

5.3 Activities

Typical activities include:

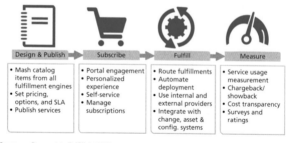

Design & Publish	Subscribe	Fulfill	Measure
• Mash catalog items from all fulfillment engines • Set pricing, options, and SLA • Publish services	• Portal engagement • Personalized experience • Self-service • Manage subscriptions	• Route fulfillments • Automate deployment • Use internal and external providers • Integrate with change, asset & config. systems	• Service usage measurement • Chargeback/ showback • Cost transparency • Surveys and ratings

Figure 30: Request to Fulfill Activities

5.4 Value Stream Diagram

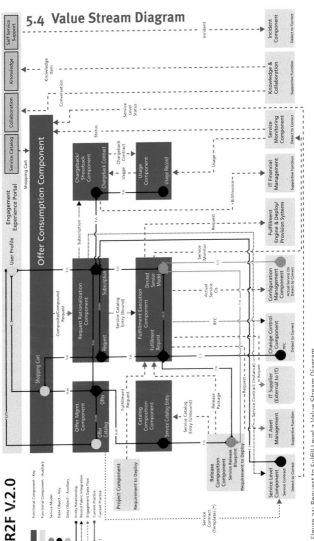

Figure 31: Request to Fulfill Level 2 Value Stream Diagram

5.5 Engagement Experience Portal

 The Engagement Experience Portal is a Secondary Functional Component; refer to *Functional Component* within Section 2.3.3.

5.5.1 Purpose

The Engagement Experience Portal facilitates service consumption by connecting any potential consumer with the right information, goods, services, or capability at the right time through a single experience, taking into account the consumer profile. It is based on a system of engagement design pattern where consumers access different functional components through a common user experience.

Through the Engagement Experience Portal, the consumer has access to self-service support functionalities like community and collaboration, knowledge associated with services, information about consumed services and service status.

5.5.2 Key Data Objects

The **User Profile** data object contains personal data associated with a specific user and the explicit digital representation of a person's identity.

The key attributes are: UserID, UserName, Role.

5.5.3 Key Data Object Relationships

User Profile to Offer Catalog (n:m): Presents a personalized list of offers from the catalog depending on the consumer profile.

User Profile to Shopping Cart (1:1): Establishes the link between the catalog items, which are ordered, and the consumer and helps to identify the authorized person where an approval is required.

Model

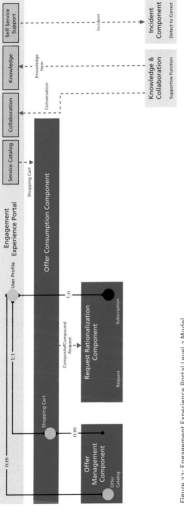

Figure 32: Engagement Experience Portal Level 2 Model

User Profile to Subscription (1:n): Creates a link between the user and a subscription for every service where a Subscription is required.

5.5.4 Main Functions

The Engagement Experience Portal functional component is available to all users that desire to consume IT services. It exposes various IT functions and capabilities in a single place, unifying the experience. It allows consumers to manage their User Profile (to varying degrees as some attributes may be provider-controlled).

The Engagement Experience Portal also includes the following sub-components:

- The Service Catalog functional sub-component enables consumers to engage with and consume services through the Offer Consumption functional component.
- The Collaboration functional sub-component provides the user front end for an enterprise collaboration experience, such as a chat capability.
- The Knowledge functional sub-component provides the interface for users to search and read knowledge data objects of all types and sources.
- The Self-Service Support functional sub-component provides service consumers with a way to address more of their IT-related issues, as well as receive information regarding their existing records without necessarily engaging IT providers. It enables users to create new support tickets, view and update their existing support tickets and access the Knowledge data objects.

5.6 Offer Consumption Functional Component

5.6.1 Purpose

The Offer Consumption functional component presents consumable offers derived from Service Catalog Entries with associated descriptions, pictures, prices, and purchasing options to prospective consumers. It facilitates consumption/management of and payment for IT services rendered. It enables consumers to manage their subscriptions.

5.6.2 Key Data Objects

The **Shopping Cart** data object contains the IT services that the user wants to order; the object only exists during the actual shopping session.

The key attributes are: ShoppingCartID, UserID, ApproverID, Status. And for every item in the Shopping Cart: LineItem, offerID, ReqValue.

5.6.3 Key Data Object Relationships

Shopping Cart to User Profile (1:1): Relates the contents of the Shopping Cart relate to a specific user, who is actually ordering the services.

Shopping Cart to Offer (n:m): Presents those items available to the end-user from the existing Offers.

Shopping Cart to Request (1:n): Establishes the link between the Shopping Cart and the Requests necessary to fulfill the services ordered in the shopping experience.

5.6.4 Main Functions

The Offer Consumption functional component provides information on items users need to order from existing offers and shall provide all necessary information to guarantee the fulfillment. It also provides information on the existing Subscription to enable the user to change/cancel existing Subscriptions. It allows consumers to order multiple offers in one transaction and enables consumers to order services in behalf of other consumers.

If the Service Level functional component exists, the Offer Consumption functional component exposes information on the Service Level status for the services to which the user subscribed.

Model

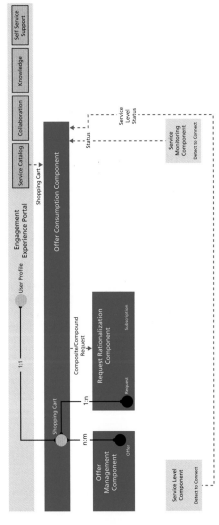

Figure 33: Offer Consumption Functional Component Level 2 Model

5.7 Offer Management Functional Component

5.7.1 Purpose

The Offer Management functional component aggregates all Catalog Composition items and external supplier catalogs into consumable offers. It builds and publishes the various offerings into Offer Catalogs for various populations. It also fulfills each Offer through numerous underlying Catalog Compositions.

5.7.2 Key Data Objects

The **Offer data** object defines how a Service Catalog Entry will be instantiated and under what terms and conditions – price, deployment, approval, workflow, service level (contract), etc.

The key attributes are: OfferID, CatalogID, OfferName, StartDate, ExpiryDate, Status, Price, ReqValue.

The **Offer Catalog** data object is a set or collection of Offers that are grouped together as something that can be consumed by certain consumers or consumer groups.

The key attributes are: CatalogID, CatalogName, ServiceID, Role.

5.7.3 Key Data Object Relationships

Offer to Service Catalog Entry (n:m): Ensures all required information is captured for the fulfillment (deployment/delivery) of the service.

Offer Catalog to Offer (n:m): Defines the collection of Offers that comprise each Offer Catalog.

Offer Catalog to User Profile (n:m): Defines which users can access/consume each Offer Catalog.

Model

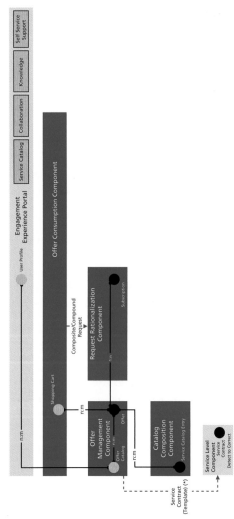

Figure 34: Offer Management Functional Component Level 2 Model

5.7.4 Main Functions

The Offer Management functional component provides all of the offers available to consumers to the Offer Consumption functional component. It allows to group services from multiple service provider (internal and external) into a single offer. It may create the Service Contract template and provide information to the Service Level functional component.

5.8 Catalog Composition Functional Component

5.8.1 Purpose

The Catalog Composition functional component creates, updates, and publishes Service Catalog Entries including all their dependencies necessary to be presented as an Offer in the Offer Management functional component.

5.8.2 Key Data Objects

The **Service Catalog Entry** data object is a Logical Service Blueprint managed by the Offer Management functional component. It is an authoritative source for the consolidated set of IT services that can be presented as Offers.

The key attributes are: ServiceID, ServiceName, ReqValue.

5.8.3 Key Data Object Relationships

Service Catalog Entry to Service Release Blueprint (1:n): Ensures all catalog entries relate to the specific service definitions used for fulfillment.

Service Catalog Entry to Offer (n:m): Ensures all information needed is captured during the order phase.

5.8.4 Main Functions

The Catalog Composition functional component manages inter-dependencies within the services.

Model

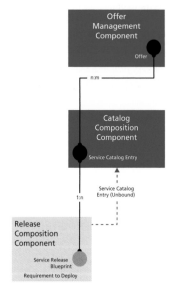

Figure 35: Catalog Composition Functional Component Level 2 Model

5.9 Request Rationalization Functional Component

5.9.1 Purpose

The Request Rationalization functional component rationalizes, breaks down, and routes "clean order" requests (ready for fulfillment) to appropriate Fulfillment Execution engines or providers in order to deliver services to consumers. This may involve breaking down a single order/ request into multiple Fulfillment Requests.

It ensures appropriate fulfillment-related Subscription information is kept up-to-date, such as approval/rejections, modifications, cancellations, and so on. It also enables the recording of patterns of service consumption that can be used to shape demand for new and/or improved services.

5.9.2 Key Data Objects

The **Request** data object contains all Offers from the Shopping Cart which have been consumed and need to be fulfilled.

The key attributes are: RequestID, UserID, Status, RequestDate, MaxFulFillDate, ActFulFillDate, OfferID, SubscriptionID, ServiceID, ReqValue.

The **Subscription** data object represents the rights to access a service that has been provided to a consumer.

The key attributes are: SubscriptionID, UserID.

5.9.3 Key Data Object Relationships

Request to Shopping Cart (1:n): Enables the traceability of Requests to the originating order (in the form of the Shopping Cart).

Request to Subscription (n:m): Enables traceability between the Request and the resulting Subscription.

Request to Fulfillment Request (1:n): Used for tracking fulfillment as well as to navigate between dependent Fulfillment Requests.

Model

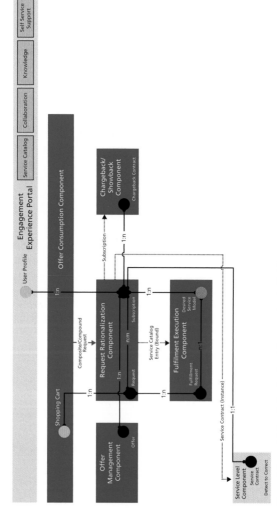

Figure 36: Request Rationalization Functional Component Level 2 Model

Subscription to User Profile (n:1): Enables the consumer to manage all of their Subscriptions.

Subscription to Offer (1:n): Provides traceability between the Subscription and the Service Contract (via the Offer).

Subscription to Chargeback Contract (1:n): Facilitates the various chargeback/showback calculations that are dependent on Subscription details such as its contract duration and service status.

Subscription to Desired Service Model (1:n): Enables traceability between the consumer, their Subscription, and the realized Service Model.

5.9.4 Main Functions

The Request Rationalization functional component provides information on the fulfillment status, information on Subscription for the associated Chargeback Contract, and information on Request delivery times for SLA measurements. It breaks down the composite request (described by the Shopping Cart and consumer-selected values) into the individual Requests that need to be fulfilled. It also sends the bound Service Catalog Entry to the Fulfillment Execution functional component.

5.10 Fulfillment Execution Functional Component

5.10.1 Purpose

The Fulfillment Execution functional component orchestrates the delivery of the various requests amongst (one or more) fulfillment engines in order to deliver the IT service.

To engage the fulfillers (systems, engaged systems, or external providers that perform actions), the Fulfillment Execution functional component manages a registry of the available fulfillers, takes the bound Service

Catalog Entry, and generates both the relevant Fulfillment Requests and the Desired Service Model data object. It updates the IT asset inventory as they are ordered. It also requests standard changes and updates the Configuration Management functional component (if needed) on delivery of components. It maintains visibility into supplier capacity levels and raises alerts if capacity appears to be insufficient for immediate demand.

The Fulfillment Execution functional component can be used via two paradigms:

- **Consumer-driven**: A consumer request results in a bound Service Catalog Entry which is broken down into the necessary Fulfillment Requests needed to fulfill the originating request.
- **Direct access** (without a Service Catalog Entry): In cases in which there aren't sufficient catalog entries to describe the fulfillment and no entries are planned to be created, the Release Composition functional component (R2D Value Stream) engages and provides enough information to the Fulfillment Execution functional component in order to create the Fulfillment Request(s) necessary to perform the actions needed.

5.10.2 Key Data Objects

The **Fulfillment Request** data object describes all fulfillment aspects of an IT service.

The key attributes are: FulfillmentID, RequestID, DesiredServiceID, RFCID, Status.

The **Desired Service Model** data object is an instantiation of the unbound Service Catalog Entry. This results in a single realized deployment for the service.

The key attributes are: DesiredServiceID, SubscriptionID, ServiceReleaseBlueprintID, ActualServiceCI_ID.

5.10.3 Key Data Object Relationships

Fulfillment Request to Request (n:1): Informs on Fulfillment Request status.

Fulfillment Request to Service Release Blueprint (n:1): Allows the Service Release Blueprint to supply the Fulfillment Request with information needed to instantiate the service.

Fulfillment Request to Desired Service Model (n:1): Acquires relevant information.

Fulfillment Request to RFC (1:1): Enables, if applicable, the RFC created to be linked to the originating Request.

Desired Service Model to Subscription (n:1): Creates the traceability from service to Subscription.

Desired Service Model to Service Release Blueprint (n:1): Acquires all necessary service information for fulfillment.

Desired Service Model to Actual Service CI (1:1): Creates traceability and enables verification of correct deployment/fulfillment.

5.10.4 Main Functions

The Fulfillment Execution functional component selects the appropriate fulfillment mechanism, coordinates if multiple fulfillment mechanisms are needed, and manages the dependencies required to fulfill the IT service request. It also provides the Subscription status to the Request Rationalization functional component. It creates the Actual Service CIs within the Configuration Management functional component. If necessary, the Fulfillment Execution functional component creates an RFC associated with the service instantiation that is created within the Change Control functional component (D2C Value Stream).

Model

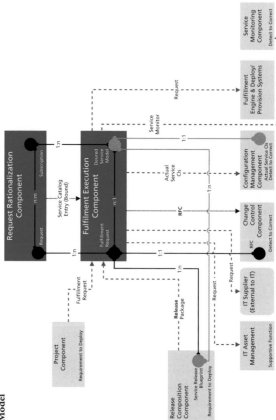

Figure 37: Fulfillment Execution Functional Component Level 2 Model

The Fulfillment Execution functional component can:

- Create or modify a service monitor for the service provided in the Request as part of fulfillment.
- Create/route a Request to an external service provider to fulfill part or all of the service.
- Request IT assets necessary for fulfillment (such as licenses).
- Trigger deployment engines to enable fulfillment of the service.

5.7 Usage Functional Component

5.7.1 Purpose
The Usage functional component tracks actual usage of subscribed IT services by gathering IT service usage metrics, activity, and history. It processes and breaks down usage information for each subscription, its consumers, providers, etc.

5.7.2 Key Data Objects
The **Usage** data object is the measured use of a particular service or service component.

The key attributes are: UsageID, ChargebackContractID.

5.7.3 Key Data Object Relationships
Usage Record to Chargeback Contract (n:1): Utilized to calculate chargeback amounts in cases in which the Chargeback Contract is dependent on Usage.

5.7.4 Main Functions
The Usage functional component encrypts sensitive usage information or sets appropriate access controls. Furthermore, it generates service usage history and activity reports. It also provides usage information to

the Chargeback Contract component enabling usage-based showback or chargeback.

Model

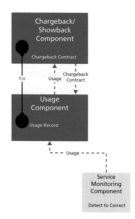

Figure 38: Usage Functional Component Level 2 Model

5.8 Chargeback/Showback Functional Component

5.8.1 Purpose

The Chargeback/Showback functional component provides chargeback or showback for services. It breaks down chargeback or showback and traces their line items to individual cost drivers based on the cost model. It also consolidates IT service Subscription (right to use) and actual Usage as the usage may differ from the right to use.

5.8.2 Key Data Objects

The **Chargeback Contract** data object details the financial obligations between the service consumer and provider(s).

The key attributes are: ChargebackContractID, SubscriptionID.

5.8.3 Key Data Object Relationships

Chargeback Contract to Subscription (n:1): Provides the traceability between the service rendered and the expected charges for those services.

5.8.4 Main Functions

The Chargeback/Showback functional component provides the price of consuming/subscribing to a service. It takes actual usage into consideration when calculating the price of consuming a service.

If an IT Financial Management component exists, the Chargeback/Showback functional component can provide the necessary information in order for the IT Financial Management supporting function to produce invoices or bills for services rendered.

Model

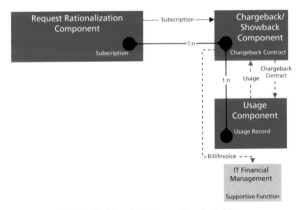

Figure 39: Chargeback/Showback Functional Component Level 2 Model

5.9 Knowledge & Collaboration Secondary Functional Component

5.9.1 Purpose

The Knowledge & Collaboration secondary component provides knowledge and conversations that help to address the needs of IT service consumers. It includes articles, conversations from users, webinars, videos, training materials, etc. It encourages users and IT staff to contribute to knowledge in order to reduce the number of requests for information/knowledge that arrive at the IT service desk.

5.9.2 Key Data Objects

The **Knowledge** data object is structured and unstructured Knowledge from the Knowledge & Collaboration functional component.

The key attributes are: KnowledgeID, AuthorID, RelatedService, ProblemID, Status, PublishDate, ExpiryDate, Title, Body.

The **Conversation** data object gathers user conversations from the Knowledge & Collaboration functional component.

The key attributes are: UserID, KnowledgeID, Body.

5.9.3 Key Data Object Relationships

Knowledge to Problem (n:m): Links a Problem to the Knowledge involved.

Knowledge to Conversation (n:m): Links a Conversation to the Knowledge involved.

5.9.4 Main Functions

The Knowledge & Collaboration component enables SMEs to submit and/or approve Knowledge data objects. It provides functionality to enable the IT service consumers and IT staff to rank Knowledge data objects and Conversations. It also provides functionality to enable IT service consumers to participate in Conversations relating to the IT services they consume. Furthermore, it can aggregate multiple Knowledge sources.

Model

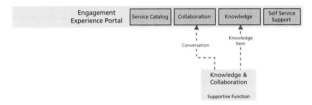

Figure 40: Knowledge & Collaboration Supporting Function Level 2 Model

Chapter 6
The D2C Value Stream

This chapter describes the Detect to Correct (D2C) Value Stream.

6.1 Overview
The Detect to Correct (D2C) Value Stream:
- Brings together IT service operations to enhance results and efficiency
- Enables end-to-end visibility using a shared configuration model
- Identifies issues before they affect users
- Reduces the MTTR

The Detect to Correct (D2C) Value Stream provides a framework for integrating the monitoring, management, remediation, and other operational aspects associated with realized services and/or those under construction. It also provides a comprehensive overview of the business of IT operations and the services these teams deliver. Anchored by the Service Model, the D2C Value Stream delivers new levels of insight which help improve understanding of the inter-dependencies among the various operational domains; including Event, Incident, Problem, Change Control, and Configuration Management. It also provides the business context for operational requests and new requirements. The D2C Value Stream is designed to accommodate a variety of sourcing methodologies across services, technologies, and functions. This value stream understands the inter-relationships and inter-dependencies required to fix operational issues. It supports IT business objectives of greater agility, improved uptime, and lower cost per service.

The D2C Value Stream provides a framework for bringing IT service operations functions together to enhance IT results and efficiencies. Data in each operation's domain is generally not shared with other domains because they do not understand which key data objects to share and do not have a common language for sharing. When projects are created to solve this, it is often too difficult and cumbersome to finish or there is an internal technology or organization shift that invalidates the result.

The D2C Value Stream defines the functional components and the data that needs to flow between components that enhance a business and service-oriented approach to maintenance and facilitates data flow to the other value streams.

6.2 Key Value Propositions
The key value propositions for adopting the D2C Value Stream are:
- Timely identification and prioritization of an issue.
- Improved data sharing to accelerate ability to understand the business impact.
- Automation both within domains and across domains.
- Ensuring an operating model, capabilities, and processes that can handle the complexity of service delivery across multiple internal and external domains.
- Effective linkage of Events to Incidents to Problems to Defects in the R2D Value Stream.

6.3 Activities
Typical activities include:

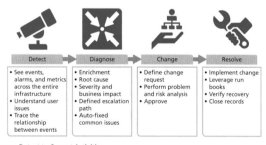

Figure 41: Detect to Correct Activities

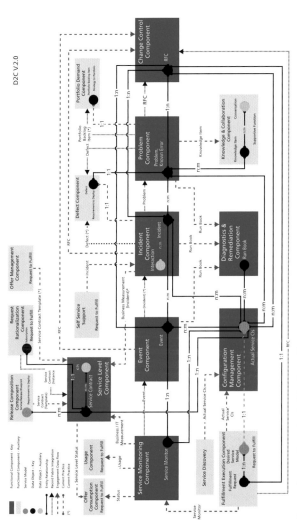

Figure 42: Detect to Correct Level 2 Value Stream Diagram

6.4 Service Monitoring Functional Component

6.4.1 Purpose

The Service Monitoring function component is in charge of creating, running, and managing monitors, which measure all aspects/layers of a service such as infrastructure (system and network), application, and security.

6.4.2 Key Data Objects

The **Service Monitor** data object performs the operational measurement aspects of a CI or an IT service.

The key attributes are: ServiceMonitorID, Name, Description, Type, MeasurementDefinitions, LastRunTime, LastRunStatus, ActualServiceCI_ID.

6.4.3 Key Data Object Relationships

Service Monitor to Event (1:n): Enables traceability from the Events that are created to the Service Monitor from which they originated.

Service Monitor to Actual Service CIs (1:n): Identifies the CI being monitored.

6.4.4 Main Functions

The main functions of the Service Monitoring functional component are to:
- Be the system of records for all Service Monitors.
- Manage the lifecycle of the Service Monitor.
- Perform monitoring of all aspects of an IT service.
- Store all the results of the measurement being done.
- Calculate results of compound Service Monitors.

If an Event functional component exists, the Service Monitoring functional component initiates the creation of an Event or alert that is passed to the Event functional component.

If an Offer Consumption functional component exists, the Service Monitoring functional component can provide service monitoring status.

If a Usage functional component exists, the Service Monitoring functional component can provide service usage measurements.

If a Service Level component exists, the Service Monitoring functional component can provide business/IT measurements.

If a Fulfillment Execution functional component exists, the Service Monitoring functional component can receive Service Monitor definitions.

Model

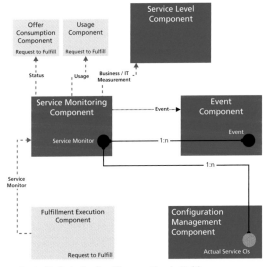

Figure 43: Service Monitoring Functional Component Level 2 Model

6.5 Event Functional Component

6.5.1 Purpose

The Event functional component manages Events through the Event lifecycle for events that occur on any IT service.

6.5.2 Key Data Objects

The **Event** data object represents an alert/notification signifying a change of state of a monitored CI.

The key attributes are: EventID, Name, Category, EventType, EventStatus, EvetnStatusTime, Severity, ThresholdDéfinitions, AssignedTo, IsCorrelated, ActualServiceCI_ID.

6.5.3 Key Data Object Relationships

Event to Incident (n:m): Enables the connection between the Incidents and Events.

Event to RFC (1:n): Associates an Event for the RFC processing.

Event to Actual Service CIs (n:m): Identifies Actual Service CIs associated with the Event(s).

Service Monitor to Event (1:n): Enables traceability from the Events that are created to the Service Monitor from which they originated.

6.5.4 Main Functions

The main functions of the Event Functional Component are:
- Be the system of record for all Events.
- Manage the state and lifecycle of the Events.
- Manage the correlation between Events.
- Categorize Event data.

- Forward Events categorized as Incidents to the Incident functional component.
- Initiate eventually a change request (RFC) based on Event data to the Change Control functional component.
- Create an association between the Event data object and the related Actual Service CI(s).

If a Diagnostics & Remediation functional component exists, the Event functional component may send Events for diagnostics and remediation processing.

Model

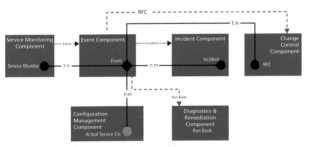

Figure 44: Event Functional Component Level 2 Model

6.6 Incident Functional Component

6.6.1 Purpose

The Incident functional component facilitates normal service operations restoration as quickly as possible and minimizes the impact on business operations, thus optimizing service quality and availability.

An Incident is defined as an unplanned interruption to an IT service or reduction in the quality of an IT service as defined within the Service Contract related to the IT service.

An Interaction is a record of any end-user contact with the service desk agent.

6.6.2 Key Data Objects

The **Incident** data object hosts and manages Incident data.

The key attributes are: IncidentID, Category, SubCategory, IncidentStatus, IncidentStatusTime, Severity, Priority, Title, Description, AssignedTo, ActualServiceCI_ID.

The **Interaction** data object hosts the record of an end-user's contact with the service desk.

The key attribute is: InteractionID.

6.6.3 Key Data Object Relationships

- **Incident to Problem, Known Error** (n:m): Establishes connection between the Incidents that are converted to Problems.
- **Incident to RFC** (1:n): Connects RFCs to the Incidents from which they originated.
- **Incident to Defect** (1:1): Determines there is a need for an emergency fix from development.
- **Incident to Actual Service CIs** (n:m): Identifies CI to which the Incident is associated and usually the main subject of.
- **Event to Incident** (n:m): Enables the connection between the Incidents and Events.

6.6.4 Main Functions

The main functions of the Incident Functional Component are:
- Be the system of record for all Incidents.
- Manage the state escalation paths and general lifecycle of the Incident.
- Allow an Incident to be initiated from an Event.

- Create an Incident when an Interaction cannot be associated with an existing Incident because it requires additional clarification, diagnostics, or support actions.
- Create an association between the Incident data object and the related Actual Service CI(s).

If a Defect functional component exists, the Incident functional component may initiate the creation of a Defect when Incident diagnostics determines that an emergency fix is required from development for resolution. The Defect is created and forwarded to the Defect functional component in the R2D Value Stream.

If a Diagnostics & Remediation functional component exists, the Incident functional component can trigger the execution of a Run Book (either automated or manual) to provide diagnostic information or remediation steps.

If a Problem functional component exists, the Incident functional component may create a Problem record when the Incident is severe, requires further deep investigation, or is repeating.

If a Change Control functional component exists, the Incident functional component can trigger the creation of an RFC in order to implement a fix to the Incident fault.

If a Self-Service Support functional component (R2F Value Stream) exists, the Incident functional component can allow the initiation of an Interaction or an Incident.

If a Service Level functional component exists, the Incident functional component can provide business measurements of Incident data.

Model

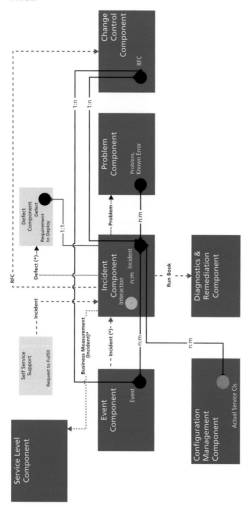

Figure 45: Incident Functional Component Level 2 Model

6.7 Problem Functional Component

6.7.1 Purpose

The Problem functional component is responsible for managing the lifecycle of all Problems. The objectives of the Problem functional component are to solve severe/repeating Incidents, prevent Incidents from happening, and minimize the impact of Incidents that cannot be prevented.

6.7.2 Key Data Objects

The **Problem, Known Error** data object defines the Problem or Known Error and manages the Problem and Known Error lifecycle.

The key attributes are: ProblemID, Category, SubCategory, ProblemStatus, ProblemStatusTime, Title, Description, AsssignedTo, ActualServiceCI_ID.

6.7.3 Key Data Object Relationships

Problem, Known Error to RFC (1:n): Enables the relation of an RFC record that is created when problem resolution requires a change.

Problem, Known Error to Portfolio Backlog Item (1:1): Ensures a Portfolio Backlog Item is created for Problems requiring a future fundamental/big fix/enhancement to the IT service.

Problem, Known Error to Defect (1:1): Enables the creation of Defects when emergency/specific fixes require development.

Incident to Problem, Known Error (n:m): Establishes connection between the Incidents that are converted to Problems.

Problem, Known Error to Actual Service CI (n:m): Identifies CI to which the Problem is associated.

Problem, Known Error to Knowledge (n:m): Creates a relationship between the Knowledge data object and the Problem from which it originated.

6.7.4 Main Functions

The main functions of the Problem Functional Component are:

- Be the system of record for all Problem records.
- Manage the state and lifecycle of the Problem.
- Associate Problem(s) to CI(s).
- Create Known Error data object instances from unsolved Problems.

If a Diagnostics & Remediation functional component exists, the Problem functional component can push Problem data to trigger the execution of a Run Book data object to provide diagnostics information or remediation steps.

If a Change Control functional component exists, the Problem functional component creates an RFC associated to a Problem in order to implement a fix to the issue that is documented by the Problem.

If a Knowledge & Collaboration functional component exists, the Problem functional component uses existing Knowledge data to solve a Problem and can create a new Knowledge data object based on Problem Management activities.

If an Incident functional component exists, the Problem functional component associates Incident data to the corresponding Problem record and continues the investigation around the Incident reported fault within the Problem lifecycle.

If a Defect functional component exists, the Problem functional component pushes Problem data requiring emergency/specific development to the Defect functional component (R2D Value Stream).

If a Portfolio Demand functional component exists, the Problem functional component may push a Portfolio Backlog Item to the Portfolio Demand functional component for backlog processing.

Model

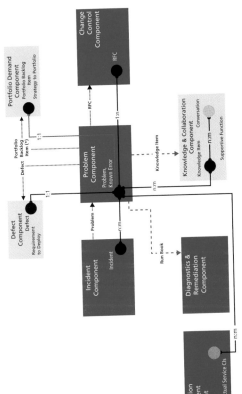

Figure 46: Problem Functional Component Level 2 Model

6.8 Change Control Functional Component

6.8.1 Purpose

The Change Control functional component is the system that is responsible for managing the lifecycle of all the RFCs in the IT environment. It makes sure that changes are done in a standardized way so that the business risk is minimized.

It manages change by facilitating communication with stakeholders and by assessing risk of proposed changes. Furthermore, it enables management of organizational changes and training needed for making a new release a success. Besides, it supports automation of changes so that human participation is minimized and uses a change calendar in order to avoid change conflicts.

6.8.2 Key Data Objects

The **RFC** data object records data required to manage the change lifecycle. An RFC includes details of the proposed change.

The key attributes are: RFCID, Category, SubCategory, ChangePhase, ChangePhaseTime, ApprovalStatus, ChangeRisk, PlannedStartTime, PlannedEndTime, Title, Description, AssignedTo, ActualServiceCI_ID.

6.8.3 Key Data Object Relationships

- **Fulfillment Request to RFC** (1:1): Identifies the Fulfillment Request from the Fulfillment Execution functional component (R2F Value Stream) that will create an RFC on service implementation/ instantiation.
- **RFC to Actual Service CIs** (n:m): Associates the RFC with affected CI(s).
- **Problem, Known Error to RFC** (1:n): Enables the relation of an RFC record that is created when problem resolution requires a change.

- **Incident to RFC** (1:n): Connects RFCs to the Incidents from which they originated.
- **RFC to Event** (1:n): Associates an Event that is available for RFC processing.

6.8.4 Main Functions

The Change Control functional component acts as an authoritative system of record for all change request information. It manages the state and lifecycle of the change and associate change(s) to CI(s). It can also provide change data to the Event and/or Service Monitoring functional components in the context of change impact analysis.

If an Incident functional component exists, the Change Control functional component associates changes with Incidents bi-directionally.

If an Event functional component exists, the Change Control functional component may associate changes with Events when a change triggers an Event or an Event occurs during a change period.

If a Fulfillment Execution functional component exists, the Change Control functional component associates the Fulfillment Request with the RFC record as the overall framework that facilitates the IT service implementation/instantiation.

If a Problem functional component exists, the Change Control functional component associates RFCs to the Problem in order to implement a fix to the issue that is documented by the Problem.

Model

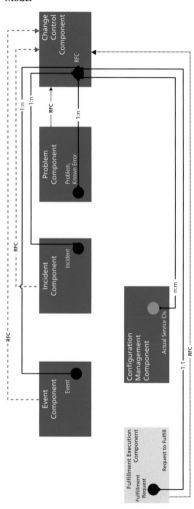

Figure 47: Change Control Functional Component Level 2 Model

6.9 Configuration Management Functional Component

6.9.1 Purpose

The Configuration Management functional component is focused on tracking the inventories of Actual Service CIs and their associated relationships. It identifies, controls, records, reports, audits, and verifies service CIs.

6.9.2 Key Data Objects

The **Actual Service CI** data object serves as the data store for the realization of the service in the production environment. A CI is defined as any component that may need to be managed in order to deliver an IT service.

The key attributes are: ActualServiceCI_ID, Name, Type, CreateTime, LastModifiedTime, Owner, Location.

6.9.3 Key Data Object Relationships

- **RFC to Actual Service CIs** (n:m): Associates the RFC with affected CI(s).
- **Problem, Known Error to Actual Service CI** (n:m): Identifies the CI to which the Problem is associated.
- **Run Book to Actual Service CI** (n:m): Maps Run Book records to the associated CIs.
- **Incident to Actual Service CIs** (n:m): Identifies the CI to which the Incident is associated and usually the main subject of.
- **Event to Actual Service CIs** (n:m): Identifies the Actual Service CI associated with the Event (s).
- **Actual Service CIs to Service Contract** (1:n): Ensures functional component and data object traceability in the value stream.
- **Service Monitor to Actual Service CIs** (1:n): Identifies the CI being monitored.

6.9.4 Main Functions

The Configuration Management functional component is the system of record for all Actual Service CIs and their associated relationships. It manages the lifecycle of the CI and allows hierarchical relationships between CIs. Moreover, it serves as the data store for the realization of the service in the production environment.

If a Diagnostics & Remediation functional component exists, the Configuration Management functional component associates a Run Book with the CI against which the Run Book is associated.

If a Change Control functional component exists, the Configuration Management functional component associates a CI with an RFC with which the change is associated. It also calculates and provides the change impact based on the proposed change and the CI relationships.

If a Problem functional component exists, the Configuration Management functional component associates the CI with the Problem record against which the Problem is associated.

If an Incident functional component exists, the Configuration Management functional component associates the CI with the Incident with which the Incident is associated. It also calculates and provides the business impact of the Incident to help in the prioritization process.

If an Event functional component exists, the Configuration Management functional component associates the CI with the Event with which the change is associated. It also calculates and provides the business impact of the Event to help in the prioritization process.

If a Service Monitoring functional component exists, the Configuration Management functional component associates the CI with the Service Monitor with which the change is associated.

Model

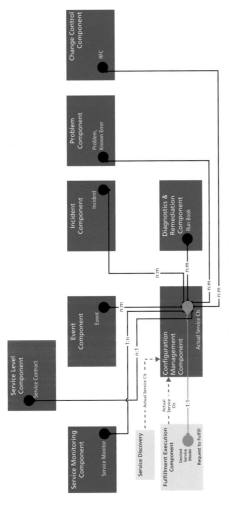

Figure 48: Configuration Management Functional Component Level 2 Model

6.10 Diagnostics & Remediation Functional Component

6.10.1 Purpose

Through the use of Run Books, the Diagnostics & Remediation functional component provides diagnostics information and/or remediation steps to shorten the MTTR. Run Books help streamline diagnostics and remediation for service functions by applying knowledge solutions to service anomalies.

6.10.2 Key Data Objects

The **Run Book** data object is a routine compilation of the procedures and operations which the administrator or operator of the system carries out.

The key attributes are: RunbookID, Description, Category, ExecutionTime, ActualServiceCI_ID.

6.10.3 Key Data Object Relationships

CI to Run Book (n:m): Enables tracking Run Books and their associated CI.

6.10.4 Main Functions

The main functions of the Diagnostics & Remediation functional component are to:

- Be the system of record for all Run Books.
- Manage the Run Book lifecycle.
- Allow hierarchical relationships between Run Books.
- Associate a Run Book with a CI.

If an Event functional component exists, the Diagnostics & Remediation functional component can allow an Event to trigger a Run Book mainly for diagnostics purposes.

If an Incident functional component exists, the Diagnostics & Remediation functional component can allow an Incident to trigger a Run Book for diagnostics or remediation purposes (remediation that does not require RFCs).

If a Problem functional component exists, the Diagnostics & Remediation functional component can allow a Problem to trigger a Run Book for remediation purposes (after an RFC has been opened).

Model

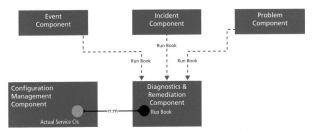

Figure 49: Diagnostics & Remediation Functional Component Level 2 Model

6.11 Service Level Functional Component

6.11.1 Purpose

The Service Level functional component enables the design, creation, and management of Service Contracts (SLAs).

6.11.2 Key Data Objects

The **Service Contract** data object describes the service characteristics and supports service measurement tracking, governance, and audit.

The key attributes are: Name, Type, Provider, Consumer, StartDate, EndDate, SupportCalendar, AdherenceCalculationPeriodicity, MaintenanceWindow, ActualServiceCI_ID.

The **Key Performance Indicator** data object defines an objective that is measured, its requested threshold, and the calculation method to be used.

The key attributes are: KeyPerformanceIndicatorName, KeyPerformanceIndicatorDescription, KeyPerformanceIndicatorThreshold.

6.11.3 Key Data Object Relationships

Service Release Blueprint to Service Contract (n:m): Identifies the Service Release Blueprint where the Service Contract templates are being stored.

Actual Service CIs to Service Contract (1:n): Ensures functional component and data object traceability in the value stream.

Service Contract to KPI (n:m): Tracks the measurements associated with Service Contracts.

Subscription to Service Contract (1:1): Allows to trigger the instantiation of a Service Contract instance once a Subscription is instantiated.

6.11.4 Main Functions

The main functions of the Service Level functional component are to:
- Be a system of record for the Service Contract.
- Manage the Service Contract and the KPIs lifecycle.
- Manage the state of the Service Contract.
- Allow hierarchical relationships between Service Contracts.
- Manage the relations between the Service Contracts and the KPIs.

- Receive measurements covered by the Service Contract.
- Create reports on the Service Contracts.

If a Service Monitoring functional component exists, the Service Level functional component can receive business/IT measurements from Service Monitoring.

If a Release Composition functional component exists, the Service Level functional component can instantiate a Service Contract from a Service Release Blueprint using the Service Contract (template).

If an Offer Management functional component exists, the Service Level functional component may instantiate a Service Contract from a Service Contract (template) originating from the Offer Management functional component (R2F Value Stream).

If a Request Rationalization functional component exists, the Service Level functional component creates a Service Contract (instance) and starts measuring it once a Subscription is instantiated.

If an Incident functional component exists, the Service Level functional component may receive Incident business measurements from the Incident functional component.

If an Offer Consumption functional component exists, the Service Level functional component can send reporting data on the Service Level status.

Model

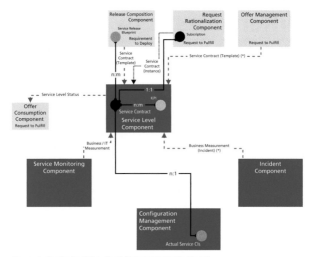

Figure 50: Service Level Functional Component Level 2 Model

6.12 Other IT Operations Area

There are other IT operations capabilities that are not part of the D2C
Value Stream but have a definite relationship with it. These include, for
example:

- Capacity planning will be reviewed in future releases.
- Availability management will be reviewed in future releases.
- Intelligence, trending, proactive alerting are within the Service
  Monitoring functional component.

Appendix A
Differences between IT4IT and ITIL

Attribute	ITIL	IT4IT Reference Architecture
Characteristics	Framework describing functions/capabilities/disciplines.	Information model-driven reference architecture that accommodates multiple process frameworks.
Origins	An aggregate of best practices drawn from a world-wide community of executives, managers, and individual contributors.	Driven by specific needs of Enterprise Architects and IT managers.
Form	Primarily narrative.	Primarily architectural, framed using the TOGAF standard and presented using the ArchiMate language.
Utility	Oriented to education.	Solution-orientation; usable "off-the-shelf".
Value Proposition	Enable detailed analysis at the function process level.	Enables choreography of four high-level IT value streams (Strategy to Portfolio, Requirement to Deploy, Request to Fulfill, Detect to Correct) and offers prescriptive guidance for the design of products and services that deliver them.
Structure		Mutually-exclusive and comprehensive architectural catalogs.

Attribute	ITIL	IT4IT Reference Architecture
Granularity		Precise and prescriptive representation of data and integration patterns for the whole IT management domain.
Agility	Implicit waterfall, top-down planning orientation.	Explicit accommodation of agile and DevOps trends and lean Kanban approaches.
Provenance	Evolved through various proprietary ownerships.	Dynamic, open peer-to-peer development and review processes under the aegis of The Open Group.

Appendix B
Glossary

Service Lifecycle Data Object (Data Object)

Data or records produced and/or consumed to advance or control the service model as it progresses through its lifecycle phases. Data objects can take a physical or digital form and are produced, consumed, or modified by functional components. Within the IT4IT Reference Architecture there are two classifications of data objects:

- Key – those essential to managing or advancing the service lifecycle.
- Auxiliary – those important but not essential.

IT Value Chain

A classification scheme for the set of primary and supporting activities that contribute to the overall lifecycle of creating net value of a product or service offering provided by or through the IT function. Within the IT4IT framework it is used to describe the operating model for the IT business function. It includes primary activities such as planning, production, consumption, fulfillment, and support. It also includes supporting activities such as finance, human resource, governance, and supplier management.

Value Chain

A classification scheme for the complete set of primary and supporting activities that contribute to the lifecycle of creating net value of a market offering. Originates from Michael Porter's book Competitive Advantage.[2]

---

2 See the referenced M. Porter: Competitive Advantage: Creating and Sustaining Superior Performance.

Value Stream

Describes the key activities for a discreet area within the IT Value Chain where some unit of net value is created or added to the service as it progresses through its lifecycle. The IT4IT framework describes four value streams (Strategy to Portfolio, Requirement to Deploy, Request to Fulfill, Detect to Correct).

Functional Component

A software building block. The smallest unit of technology in the IT4IT Reference Architecture that can stand on its own and be useful as a whole to an IT practitioner (or IT service provider). Functional components must have defined inputs and outputs that are data objects and it must have an impact on a key data object.

Service Model Backbone Data Object

Key data objects that annotate an aspect of the service model in its conceptual, logical, or physical state. These data objects and their relationships form the Service Model Backbone which provides a holistic view of a service.

Relationship

Primarily used to depict the connections between (or interactions with) data objects. In the IT4IT Reference Architecture, relationships are based on three design principles:

- System of record – used to depict the relationships used to control authoritative source data via a system-to-system interface. These relationships are prescriptive in that they must be maintained to ensure the integrity of the IT4IT Reference Architecture.
- System of engagement – used to describe the relationships between data objects and humans or functional components via a user experience interface.

- System of insight – used to describe relationships between data objects for the purpose of generating knowledge, information, or analytics.

System of Record

A synonym for a system that contains and/or controls authoritative source data.

Note: This term can be easily confused with system of record relationships.

IT Initiative

Any one of the class of temporary endeavors such as projects or programs with a defined beginning and end, undertaken to achieve an objective or outcome, at a specified cost.

Appendix C
Acronyms and
Abbreviations

ARTS	Association for Retail Technology Standards
BIAN	Banking Industry Architecture Network
BRM	Business Risk Management
BYOD	Bring Your Own Device
CI	Configuration Item
CMMI	Capability Maturity Model Integration
COBIT	Control Objectives for Information and Related Technology
COTS	Commercial Off-The-Shelf
DevOps	Development and Operations
DML	Definitive Media Library
EMMM	Exploration, Mining, Metals & Minerals (The Open Group)
eTOM	Business Process Framework (TM Forum)
IaaS	Infrastructure as a Service
IT	Information Technology
ITIL	Information Technology Infrastructure Library
KPI	Key Performance Indicator
MTTR	Mean Time To Repair
NRF	National Retail Federation
OpEx	Operating Expenditure
PaaS	Platform as a Service
PMO	Project Management Office
QA	Quality Assurance
RFC	Request for Change
ROI	Return On Investment
SaaS	Software as a Service
SAFe	Scaled Agile Framework

SLA	Service-Level Agreement
SME	Subject Matter Expert
TOSCA	Topology and Orchestration Specification for Cloud Applications (OASIS)
UML	Unified Modeling Language

Index

T

U